Thames Estua

DESERT ISLAND BOOKS

www.desertislandbooks.com

Desert Island Local Studies

Thames Estuary Trail	1-874287-45-7
Great Men of Essex	1-874287-41-4
Essex in 1950	1-874287-42-2

Desert Island Travels

The Virgin Whore: Tiananmen, Travels & Traumas	1-874287-23-6
To Dream of Pigs: Travels in South & North Korea	1-874287-34-1

Desert Island Football Histories

Aberdeen: The European Era	1-874287-11-2
The Book of Football: A History to 1905-06	1-874287-13-9
Bristol City: The Modern Era	1-874287-28-7
Cambridge United: The League Era	1-874287-32-5
The Story of the Celtic 1888-1938	1-874287-15-5
Colchester United: From Graham to Whitton	1-874287-27-9
Coventry City: The Elite Era	1-874287-03-1
Coventry City: An Illustrated History	1-874287-36-8
England: The Quest for the World Cup	1-897850-40-9
History of the Everton Football Club 1878-1928	1-874287-14-7
Halifax Town: From Ball to Lillis	1-874287-26-0
Hereford United: The League Era	1-874287-18-X
Ireland: The Quest for the World Cup	1-897850-80-8
Ipswich Town: The Modern Era	1-874287-43-0
Luton Town: The Modern Era	1-874287-05-8
Luton Town: An Illustrated History	1-874287-37-6
Peterborough United: The Modern Era	1-874287-33-3
Peterborough United: A Who's Who	1-874287-48-1
Plymouth Argyle: 101 Golden Greats	1-874287-47-3
Portsmouth: From Tindall to Ball	1-874287-25-2
Portsmouth: Champions of England 1948-49 & 49-50	1-874287-38-4
The Story of the Rangers 1873-1923	1-874287-16-3
Red Dragons in Europe	1-874287-01-5
The Romance of the Wednesday	1-874287-17-1
Scotland: The Quest for the World Cup	1-897850-50-6
Stoke City: The Modern Era	1-874287-39-2
Stoke City: 101 Golden Greats	1-874287-46-5
Watford: An Illustrated History	1-874287-49-X
West Ham: The Elite Era	1-874287-31-7
Wimbledon: From Southern League to Premiership	1-874287-09-0
Wimbledon: From Wembley to Selhurst	1-874287-20-1
Wimbledon: The Premiership Years	1-874287-40-6

The Desert Island Dracula Library

Dracula: Sense & Nonsense	1-874287-24-4
Dracula Unearthed (annotated)	1-874287-12-0
The Lady of the Shroud (annotated)	1-874287-22-8
The Shoulder of Shasta (annotated)	1-874287-30-9
The Primrose Path	1-874287-21-X
Dracula: The Shade and the Shadow	1-874287-10-4
Dracula: The Novel & the Legend	1-874287-44-9
The Origins of Dracula	1-874287-07-4
Treatise on Vampires and Revenants	1-874287-06-6
The Jewel of Seven Stars (annotated)	1-874287-08-2
Snowbound: The Record of a Theatrical Touring Party (annotated)	1-874287-29-5
A Glimpse of America	1-874287-35-X

Thames Estuary Trail

A Walk Round the End of the World

Tom King

Desert Island Books

First Published in 2001

DESERT ISLAND BOOKS LIMITED
89 Park Street, Westcliff-on-Sea, Essex SS0 7PD
United Kingdom
www.desertislandbooks.com

© 2001 Tom King

The right of Tom King to be identified as author
of this work has been asserted by him under
The Copyright Designs and Patents Act 1988

British Library Cataloguing-in-Publication Data
A catalogue record for this book is available from
the British Library

ISBN 1-874287-45-7

Printed by ColourBooks Ltd,
Dublin, Republic of Ireland

Contents

		Page
	PREFACE	6
1	ESTUARY BLUES	7
2	BLAZED ANY GOOD TRAILS LATELY?	27
3	FOULNESS – MYSTERY ISLAND	46
4	SHOEBURY – THE NAME OF THE NOSE	67
5	SOUTHEND – THE TEEMING MUD	85
6	LEIGH, HADLEIGH – AND LOST	114
7	THE TILBURY DREAMERS	138
8	GRAVESEND DISCOVERED	156
9	DICKENS' COUNTRY	178
10	ALLHALLOWS – THAMES GHOST-TOWN	199
11	SHEPPEY – WORLD'S END	209

Preface

The Thames Estuary ought to be a success story. Here, after all, is the last flourish of Old Father Thames. It offers the traveller history, beauty, majesty, all wrapped round one of the most famous names on earth.

Instead, the Estuary lies neglected and despised. Half a million people live close to its shores. Almost all of them have turned their backs on it. It is, indeed, Britain's most massive backwater. Even the great ships that command these waters remain detached and aloof from the landscape.

The nation's ramblers have also studiously avoided the Estuary. While the much-vaunted Thames footpath covers the upper reaches of the river from London to its source, nobody has ever attempted to walk the complete circuit of the Estuary's shores.

Nobody, that is, until local journalist Tom King set out to find – or if necessary, blaze – a trail round the Estuary's edge. "I wanted," he writes, "to discover just how much I didn't know about my own backyard."

Beginning the journey on the top secret "James Bond Island" of Foulness, the author followed the 83-mile route along the Essex and Kent shores, to Warden Point on the Isle of Sheppey, the last lonely outpost of the Thames.

As he discovered and recalled the people and places of the Estuary, something unexpected happened. "I fell in love with it," he writes, with astonishment.

Just how and why this unlooked-for affair developed, along with the strange and mighty secrets contained in that mighty world of mud and water, are the unfolding themes of *Thames Estuary Trail*.

The tales brought back from these wanderings offer many revelations about this great unknown of the British landscape – the unexpected wilderness that leads to the heart of London.

CLIVE LEATHERDALE
DESERT ISLAND BOOKS

One

Estuary Blues

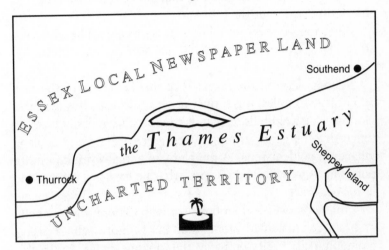

IN THE SUMMER of the new century, feeling rather sorry for the Thames Estuary, I took a long, difficult but ultimately quite eventful walk round the edge. I don't suppose it did the poor body of water much good, but in the process something rather unexpected happened. I fell in love with it.

This, then, may well be the first declaration of passion the Thames Estuary has ever received in print. It has always had a bad press – when, indeed, it has had any sort of press at all. Even the conservation organisation Greenpeace, which is supposed to favour wild places, has called it a "turd dump". Julius Caesar thought it was a bloody nuisance and other rude types have used phrases such as "dismal and plague-ridden", "suicidally dreary", and, somewhat obviously, "cold and wet."

Many people have committed suicide by throwing themselves into its waters. Quite a few of these, unkind rumour has it, had actually started the day in high spirits and holiday mood, and it was only the sight of the Estuary that unhinged them.

One south Essex amateur poetry and song-lyric group actually meets on the Canvey sea-wall, pencils in hand. Their purpose? To acquire the desired gloomy frame of mind necessary for anybody who aspires to become poet laureate and drink all the free sherry that goes with the post.

What has gone wrong? The Estuary ought to be a success story. Here is, after all, the final flourish of the most illustrious river on earth.

Nobody slags off the rear end of the Thames. For the first 185 of its 215 miles, it is a river of sweet dreams. Rising in the glorious Cotswold hills, it spends the first fifty miles of its existence tinkling gently through deep green valleys and ancient villages of golden stone. A rambler can actually drink from its pure waters without first ensuring that he carries a latrine tent in his backpack.

Childhood over, it then flows through Oxford, the city built of brain-cell coloured stone that in its more self-agonising moments calls itself "probably the greatest university in the world" and on more average days leaves out the "probably".

Leaving Oxford with a double first in bilgewater, the Thames then hits perhaps the most glorious phase of its journey, as it glides through the Chiltern beechwoods, past mellow old redbrick towns and the mellow old red faces of retired millionaires who live along its banks. Then at Windsor, it becomes a truly Royal river, with the towers of a royal fortress for its crown. The turrets of Windsor Castle descend to its banks, and at midnight the ghost of Queen Victoria may be observed, performing the rather undignified butterfly stroke in the river as she never felt able to do in life. For over a mile, the river becomes a private royal reserve. Trespassing ramblers are likely to find themselves piked where the sun don't shine by vigilant Beefeaters.

And then, of course, there is London – flower of cities all, capital city, home of government and finance, where the Thames, royal, educated, beautiful and now rich, flows past Big

Ben, the Globe Theatre, the Inns of Court, the Tower of London, Tower Bridge, Greenwich, not to mention the hush-hush twelve-storey headquarters of the Secret Service (knock three times and ask for James, the milkmen will tell you). And all of this mighty and historic city exists in the first place because of the Thames.

What a career for a river! Eat your heart out old Man Nile. Get lost, Amazon. No wonder they call the Rhine the river of whine. "Besides me," snorts the Thames, "even the Mississippi is just a muddy puddle with pretensions."

Thus, confident, dignified, and inspiring, the Great British river heads for the open sea and his final flourish of glory. "Old Father Thames keeps rolling along, down to the mighty sea," sang the baritone Peter Dawson with 27-piece orchestra and a celestial choir from Birmingham, in a record that once sold by the hundredweight.

And then, just where the heavenly choirs should be at their most wailing and Peter Dawson's voice rising to a farewell falsetto, Old Father Thames all goes horribly wrong. Instead of ascending into the heavens in some celestial reverse-waterfall, he turns into a dirty old man.

The reasons for this sad decline are numerous. They include industrialisation, Essex, excessive mud, the time-honoured habit of dumping anything that London doesn't want into or next to the Estuary, and those amateur sewage disposal techniques that turn Greenpeace red with rage.

Long before the modern age, however, even long before the first guidebook to the Thames studiously ignored the final forty per cent of the river, the Thames Estuary was recognised as an area to be shunned. The reason for this was the terrible marsh fever, known as "ague".

Outsiders unwise enough to try to settle here tended to leave fairly promptly, and usually horizontally. True, those with a marsh ancestry might survive. But Estuary folk tended to be rodent-like creatures with fish-scale skin, prone to convulsions

and slavering. Outsiders seldom made contact, let alone children with them. Even the blindest of seducers was unlikely to
cuddle up to a marsh person and whisper: "I don't half fancy
you."

The Victorians invented drainage and made the expansion
of towns like Southend and Gravesend feasible. They did this
with some relish, even planning a sort of combined sewage farm
and theme park at Rawreth, close to the Thames shore. Less
happily, they also invented modern garbage, and reckoned that
the Estuary was the ideal place to chuck it. All along the shoreline are the festering dumps of used or faulty or leaky consumer
items, the things that Londoners have chucked out, often with
a curse, starting in the nineteenth century with canvas con-
doms.

More than any other factor, it is perhaps the huge size of the
Thames Estuary that turns it into the world's wallflower. In
central London, a reasonable South African or Australian
cricketer, even if not a native one, could toss a ball from one
bank to the other, although, as you would expect from a foreigner, he would be infringing about 650 different City bye-laws
in the process.

Yet by the time the river passes Hope Reach, fifteen miles
downstream, the naked eye can't make out a human figure on
the far bank. The royal river has become a place of vast, indif-
ferent horizons, a great, grey, lowering inland sea. As a visitor
from East London is supposed to have remarked: "It scares the
cor blimey out of yer. Give me Hackney horse trough any day."

Even when it plays a momentous historic role, the Estuary
tends to be ignored. In the days before D-Day, 1944, the largest
fleet in history mustered in the Estuary, ready to service the
Normandy invasion force with fuel and ammunition. One day
it was there, the next, Southend woke up to find that this
Armada had disappeared. But Southenders were used to people
disappearing overnight, particularly when there was a landlady
and a spot of rent involved, and anyway, this was wartime, peo-

ple had other things to think about. So the extraordinary conjuring trick went unreported. It was only the Thames Estuary after all.

I was born and brought up on a ridge just north of the Estuary, and for much of my working life I have covered the area as a newspaperman. Yet like everybody else of the multitudes who live round its shore, I studiously failed to notice the Estuary. This can be quite a hard thing to do to sixteen billion pints of foaming water, but I managed it with, though I say it myself, some skill.

There were, of course, odd individual stories that took place on or by the Estuary – stories of flasher fishermen and lost whales, of surfboard pile-ups and unexploded World War II smart bombs which weren't smart enough to know that Germany had surrendered. There was also, of course, that hardy perennial of all south Essex horror shock sensation revelations: Southend Pier is falling down (it's still there incidentally).

Yet like some blinkered woodsman who is so busy whittling matchsticks that he doesn't even realise he lives in a forest, I never ever raised my eyes to the Estuary as a whole. In the end, I reckon the Estuary just got tired of waiting and decided to take matters into its own saltwater fingers.

On a Saturday in the late 1980s, I was attending a wedding at the Alexandra Yacht Club in Southend. The club is an elegant building, mounted on wooden pillars, set into the cliff-face. Every few years, the building slithers down a couple of feet, like a cautious trainee skier. It comes to rest intact, but the shock suddenly makes it look a lot older. Right now, however, after half a dozen glasses of nuptial fizz, it felt more as if the yacht club was mincing from side to side.

The moment that changed my life happened slap in the middle of the bride's father's speech. Fuddled though I was with spumante, the details remain etched. The bride's wedding dress was cut to reveal some fifteen inches or so of midriff. I had heard about such legendary creatures, but this was the first real life sighting. Funnily enough, at work she seemed a demure and buttoned up young lady, who kept her midriff and everything else carefully filed. It was the wedding that had changed her.

"I've watched my little girl grow up and I have to tell you it's not true what they say about Essex girls," declared the father to the guests. "I get the hump when I hear them slagged off and mothballed. You know the joke about 'Why did the Essex Girl wear her thermal vest inside out?' ..."

"'Cos she thought it made her look cool," chorused the guests.

It was the third and most repeatable Essex Girl joke that the father had made, under the guise of defending Essex maidens. At this point, his daughter lost all patience and jabbed a plastic fork into his arm. I turned round to see if the exit was still in the same place that I had left it.

Then I noticed the Estuary.

It is, in fact, hard *not* to notice the Estuary from this location. You cop a lot of waterway from the Alexandra Yacht Club. Its balcony and big picture windows take in much of the lower Thames and even some of the North Sea. It is exceedingly picturesque. Yet as usual with the Estuary, the guests were ignoring it. "Oooo, isn't it a lovely view," they intoned as they entered. Then they turned to the more alluring views of the bride and the bar in all their glory, and turned their backs on the picture window.

Now, however, there could be no more forgetting of the Estuary. The sky was grey, the air was dank, and the sun, sick of the bloody British weather, was taking a short break in Majorca. Yet on this miserable day, the waters of the Estuary had turned bright azure.

I turned to the nearest guest, Will, the editor of a trade union paper.

"Reassure me, comrade," I said. "Has my eyesight suffered

from excess imbibing of ketchup, or is the old river really turned blue."

Will turned to the window and squinted angrily through his specs across steadfast Tory country. "Search me, mate," he said. "Yeah, I suppose it looks a bit sort of bluish. Must be all that Jeyes fluid the bosses empty into it."

I gave up on Will and bent the next sympathetic ear I could find. The lady was clearly the bride's aunt.

"It's gone blue," I said.

"I know, filthy little man," she muttered. "And he promised us faithfully he'd keep the jokes clean."

"My mother-in-law came from Ilford and I want you to know she was a virgin lady when I married her ..." the bride's father was intoning.

The guests roared with delight. There were mouldy jokes and sausages on sticks to be had. Nobody wanted to look at some freak of scenery. I gave up trying to share the vision and stumbled onto the balcony by myself.

Yes, there could be no doubt about it. The Estuary had turned as blue as a film-star's contact lenses. It was unprecedented. Normally, in the case of the Thames Estuary, brown is the most glamorous colour available. What had happened? Clearly the drink carried more clout than I'd realised. It had perforated my retina. Yet everything else, the sky, the beach, the people walking along the esplanade below, had kept their normal hue. One or two, it was true, had green and purple hair. But I well knew that the old ladies of Southend, behind the times as ever, had just embraced the punk movement.

I had been looking for a way out of the wedding. But this was too good to miss. If three glasses of spumante could turn the muddy Estuary azure, what would six glasses do?

I turned away from the balcony and set off in search of more fizz. The speeches were soon over and the karaoke machine wheeled out. There was a large contingent of amateur operatic society bigwigs among the guests. "Some Enchanted Evening" rang out, followed by "You are my heart's delight", then "Where oh Where oh Where is love", sobbed by the chief bridesmaid. And all the time I pursued the man with the tray of spumantes to the point where he clearly considered that I was stalking him.

What wonders awaited out there on the Blue Lagoon, Estuary style? Formation swimming seals? Would the waters be split like the Red Sea by Moses, cutting the time for booze-trips to Calais by half an hour? The possibilities were endless.

Then the thought occurred: if the miracle spumante had this effect on me, what would others see in the Estuary. What would it do for the bride, for instance?

She, after all, had been knocking back the bubbly like somebody who took her responsibilities as pace-setter seriously. The Estuary had turned blue for me, but I was a boy. For her it would surely turn pink; shocking pink, indeed.

As soon as I could I retrieved her from a wrestling match with her brothers. "Got something I want to show you," I said, and I indicated the balcony.

Night had somehow fallen. Below us, at the bottom of the cliff, four visitors from, I think Poland, were enjoying a furious row. "There you are," I said, waving my arms at the pink Estuary. "The shape of your romantic destiny."

But the Estuary wasn't pink. It wasn't even blue any more. The tide had gone out. Countless square miles of foul mud whispered something that sounded like "slubth, slubth" in the dark. The Estuary had reverted to style.

One of the fighting Poles tried to lift up a parking-meter bodily, the better to smite the others. A few choice words revealed that they weren't Poles after all, just incoherent locals. The bride cocked an ear in their direction.

"What? That lot? You dissin' me or something, mate?" Then, forgetting the surroundings and everything else, she asked: "What do you think of my wedding ring?" It was certainly an impressive lump of gold, but I had just gazed on an azure

Estuary, and everything else in comparison seemed dowdy.

I was just about to express this sentiment, when luckily the Estuary started to sing.

It's an old, old river, so I suppose it was appropriate that when it did take up music, it chose a song from its own, ancient era. I vaguely recognised it as a number from some sentimental old music hall turn.

"I am calling you-hoo-hoo-hoo, hoo-hoo-hoo," went the Estuary. "Across the dew-ooo-ooo-ooo, ooo-ooo-ooo."

"Hey listen to that!" I said.

"I don't want to. It's crap music," said the bride, almost in tears. "My bloody aunt's hijacked the karaoke."

"No, it's not the karaoke, it's the Est ..." I started to say. But no. If she wanted to believe that it was the karaoke singing that song, so be it. I knew better. The whole amphitheatre of the Estuary lay visible out there, from the cold North Sea to the verge of London itself, and every square yard of slime was exerting itself to get the message across. "We are calling ye-hee-hee-hee, hee-heee-heee."

If it made a sound like the Wormwood Scrubs prison choir, well, that's just exactly how you would expect the Estuary to sound. As for why it was calling me-hee-hee-hee, hee-hee-hee specifically, well, that would just have to be worked out in the fullness of time.

The musical wake-up call started to take effect six or seven days after the wedding, when I finally recovered from the spumante. It set me to doing something quite new – thinking about the Estuary.

Okay, let's get the measure of this, I thought. So the Estuary had turned blue. The blue could be put down to some freak of the light, exacerbated by drink. And it had been a very loud karaoke machine. Yet there definitely was something extraordinary sitting out there in the Estuary, and maybe it was the Estuary itself.

The Big E didn't play any more tricks for a while. As I drove around the newspaper patch, I'd stop the car every now and then to look at it. I'd take it by surprise, suddenly swinging around on my heels to see if it was indulging in a quick two-second blue period. I tried singing "I am calling you hoo-hoo-hoo" back to it, and it was amazing how many large lady police constables popped up from behind bushes along the esplanade when I did so. I watched the Estuary from the site of road traffic accidents, on first nights at local theatres. To the news editor's amazement, I asked to cover supermarket openings if the shop in question was anywhere near the Estuary. But there were no further attempts to collar my attention. The Estuary just swilled and slurped and looked grey about the gills, even – or especially – on sunny days, in its old accustomed way.

Yet the new-found fascination did not go away. I started to collect together Amazing Facts and Figures concerning this neglected body of water. Did you know that more than half a million people live within sight of its shoreline? That until the mid-1960s more vessels passed the end of Southend Pier than any other marine site on earth? That it is the biggest classified nature reserve in England? That nobody in history has ever caught a fish off the end of Southend Pier – at least while I've been watching?

I started to look for books about the Estuary. There were plenty of volumes about the Thames as a whole, books with titles like *Sweet Thames Run Softly* or the *Little Book of the Royal River*. I lost count of the number of authors who had written up their voyages along the upper Thames. But they always seemed to stop the journeys in London. This is possibly because if you're an author from Belgravia with a name like Gay Rose you don't thumb a lift from a lighterman.

I also started to ponder my own past encounters with the Estuary. One especially bizarre episode stood out.

In June 1982 a wealthy and powerful Italian banker hanged himself from the stanchions of Blackfriars Bridge in London. Calvi was responsible for the Vatican's finances, so the world and all its media were soon buzzing with conspiracy theories.

Three or four days later, the ripples of the Calvi affair came to rest at a small, struggling local newspaper in the Essex suburbs. I was seated in the Railway Tavern with one newspaper editor and half a dozen or so fellow reporters, vaguely wondering whether the new management, who had just bought the newspaper, would insist that we work in the office, rather than the pub. We could always strike if they did, but somehow it was hard to envisage massive backing for our cause from the general public, or a nationwide sympathy strike across the railway system.

"Call for you, Tel," shouted the landlord to the editor.

His editorship found his way to the telephone on the bar, spent several animated minutes on the phone, and re-emerged amongst us, puffing with excitement.

"That was my mate on the *Mirror* and he's got a big one for us," he said. "Know that Italian geezer what got necked by a hitman near the Black Friar's pub where they do the bent sausage rolls? Well, the guy what done him got done himself, by one of those mobsters in the Vatican.

"Well," he continued, "my informant tells me that, when this assassin who was paid to assassinate the assassin had done the dirty deed, he chucked the body in the river at Tilbury."

"Was he all dressed up in Swiss Guard's gear at the time?" one reporter ventured to ask.

"That's just being silly," snapped Tel. "Now, that hitman's body – or if we're really lucky, it might even be a hit woman, with big knockers – is bobbing around in the water somewhere in Tel's patch, and Tel wants his boys and girls to find that corpse and ..." he choked back the temptation to say "interview it."

"... And, like, be first with the story."

"Come on Tel," said the chief reporter. "Even if there is some sort of body, the river police will have got it. And if they don't find it, it'll just wash up on Pig Island like all the others."

"That's not what my mate on the *Mirror* says," said Tel. "You know what the bastard said? He said: 'You Essex blokes have got so many bodies knocking round that Estuary of yours that you don't take any notice of them.' Bloody slur I call it."

"Come on Tel, you don't want to let him get to you," said the chief reporter.

"If things are getting to me," said the editor, "there is a reason. He slapped an A4 dossier in front of us. "This," he said glumly, though also with a faint measure of pride, "is something new from America called a Management Implementation Action Plan.

"And this," he said, producing last week's copy of the paper, "is one crap lead story. 'Garage roof burnt out in fire.' The fire officer stated: 'Mr Harvey is very lucky to have saved most of his garage roof.' However, neighbour, Mr Richard Waits, said: 'It wouldn't really have mattered, he was going to turn it into a granny-flat in two years time anyway.'"

There was an awkward pause while we pondered the bottom of our glasses and thought about dole queues. We knew what Tel was on about.

"Now," Tel continued, "I want some decent old-fashioned murders and cablecar crashes and Elvis Croaks It stories. Otherwise what this report says is: Local newspaper croaks it. Get my drift. I want stories like they get in the nationals. If we're going to have a fire as the front page lead I want it to be the civic centre that burns down, not some tin garage."

"Tin doesn't burn," I pointed out, helpfully.

It was definitely the wrong thing for a junior reporter to say, which was why I found myself later that afternoon on corpse-hunting duty.

"Don't come back without at least one good dead body, or you'll be one," had been one of the editor's more friendly instructions.

The scheme looked simple enough on the map. It required a slow walk down-river from Coalhouse Fort to Mucking Flats, with eyes and nose constantly pointed at the river. Sight, smell and hearing all had to be brought into play. Older reporters who had been on body hunts with the police were able to give some advice. "Listen out for the sound of flies," I was told. "If more than one bluebottle settles on your nose you've hit pay-dirt, matey."

If I saw what looked at first sight like a body, I should first call: "Are you alright, mate," three times, since nothing annoys anglers and courting couples more than to be mistaken for a cadaver. Above all, I was warned, don't try to give the kiss of life to a mud-caked body, because you may end up applying your efforts to the wrong end.

I set off in high enough spirits. Of course, one had to be realistic. The chances of finding a member of the criminal classes floating eyes-down were on the face of it slim. Yet there was hope. Plenty of bodies had been dumped into the river with concrete waistcoats, one had been told. And there had been much in the press recently about the poor quality concrete sold to council building projects. Buildings were cracking up. So why shouldn't concrete waistcoats also disintegrate, releasing their occupants to the surface with a speed that would give them the bends if they hadn't already ceased to breathe?

The river-bank walk was far from an easy trudge. Piles of rubbish and building rubble littered the edge. At times the path, such as it was, petered out into marshy scrub. From time to time I had to descend to the mud and schlap along the tidal margin. It was dirty and smelly – and woefully corpseless.

At least I had a standby plan. The worst-case scenario was that I wouldn't even muster so much as a drunken Russian sailor who had fallen off his poop deck. In that case, I would write the ultimate No Body story. I composed it in my mind as I walked along. "REVEALED!!! *Essex is NOT the body-strewn hell-hole of tabloid imagination. I walked twelve miles along the so-called River of Death on a working weekday and found nothing ...*"

Yet even the prospect of Scoop Reporter of the Year award couldn't deflect the sense of strange foreboding that was setting in. It wasn't just down to the complete absence of hideously mutilated bodies. There was something else. Something to do with the landscape itself. Something that was badly at fault.

A smell, perhaps? I knew about the power of the nose. I had once interviewed an Austrian aromas expert who told me: "Ze power of smell has more effect on our emotion zan any other of ze senses. Vrite zat down *now* I say and I will check it when I read the article that your write."

I took a deep breath. But no, the Estuary air was just filled with the familiar, reassuring smells of coal-smoke from the power station and Taiwanese bilge pumps. Then, with a jolt, I realised what it was. The Estuary was beautiful.

The river was strangely still, and from the Kent shore, on the far side of the river, there was a gentle rustle. Not the sort of rustle I was used to covering in local magistrates courts, when an ambitious cowhand had filched his employer's livestock. This rustle came from the tall marsh-grass on the Kent shore. It must have been a quarter of a mile across the water, a long way for such a sound to travel. But, then, there was an awful lot of marsh out there to generate the noise. It lay, flat as a caterpillar on a tyre truck, sleekly green after the recent rain. Then, four miles south, the marsh gave way to the Kentish downs. Hedgerows criss-crossed the hills, swelling every now and then into woods of oak and ash. It was an unchanged, unchanging landscape. One of the first hunter-gatherers to settle the Thames Valley, 40,000 years ago, would have recognised this landscape, just as he would have recognised my then Editor as one of his own kind.

It was all undoubtedly quite beautiful, in a way that the Thames Estuary just wasn't supposed to be. That was why I had felt so uneasy. It was the discomfort of preconceptions being dashed. The thought: "If you've got to drown, great place to do it in" came briefly to mind. However, landscapes weren't hot news, unless somebody was trying to flatten them. I had no interest in pretty scenery at the moment. What I wanted for my front page lead story was flyblown corpses, the more the merrier.

I removed my gaze from Kent, fixed it once more on the unlovely Essex mud at my feet, and carried on walking. The walk was now becoming a decided misery. River mud caked my legs up to the knees and above. Smelly and mire-plastered, I was rapidly turning into a passing resemblance of the corpse I sought. There was also something decidedly wrong with my left foot. Sharp pains shot through it every few seconds.

A few hundred yards down-river, I met the first sign of other human life I had seen all afternoon. He was clearly a treasure-hunter. As I approached, I realised that he'd obviously had some success. His metal-detector had been cast aside, and he was digging a substantial hole that was already several feet deep. About a dozen objects had been lined up alongside the rim of the hole. Some were still too caked with mud to be iden-tifiable. Other finds, including an old hot-water bottle, a wellington-boot, a souvenir tin-tray with a jagged hole in it, and, best of all, the framework of an old motor-bike, were easy to recognise.

"King – *Gazette*," I said, introducing myself. "Dug up any good corpses lately?"

"Nah, the machine doesn't register those," said the digger, apologetically. "Only metal. Mind you, we do dig into some ani-mal skeletons sometimes. I can let you have a nice rat bone if that will do you any good, my friend."

He was an amiable chap named, if I remember, Roger. I stood and chatted with him for a few minutes, glad of the chance to take the weight off my left foot. "You've had some luck today," I said. "Digging up that motor-bike and all."

Suddenly Roger wasn't quite so amiable any longer.

"That's my new bike what I came on, chum," he said.

It was time to get the foot out of the mouth pronto. "Oh, sorry mate. It's just that it's so covered with sh…"

"If that's a shitty bike," mate, he said, "then it's not because Queen bleedin Victoria buried it here, but because I bought it from an ad in your newspaper."

"Anyways," he added, "it's not my fault the bike got so much mud all over. Not my fault the Council won't build any roads around here. It's the only way I can get to me treasure holes, bikin it. You write to the Council, mate, if you think my motor looks filthy."

I left him to whinge, while I hobbled off down river again. I covered another half mile. But it was no use. Bodies or no bodies, my foot wasn't going to take much more.

So I turned round and headed back for base, dejected as only a journalist can be whose story has failed to stand up. There was even worse to come.

I soon passed my moody treasure-hunter ex-friend again. He had stopped digging and was picking bits of mud off his bike in a disconsolate way. We nodded.

"What you done with your shoe, mate?" he asked.

"What do you mean?"

He indicated my left foot. Then, and only then, did I understand why it hurt so much. Somewhere, slogging through the Thameside mud, I had lost my shoe. The mud had been so soft, and I had been so busy looking for bodies, that I hadn't even noticed it.

I shrugged and tried to look like the sort of tough guy whose attitude would be: "Shoes? Who's counting?"

"You lost it in the mud, didn't you. You won't get far without a shoe, mate. There're glass and cactus plants further up," he said, with more kindness than strict knowledge of Thameside botany. Then, suddenly, his face lit up. To his credit, he said the words without a flicker of a triumphal smile: "'Ere, I've got just the thing for you." He rummaged through his pile of dug-up junk and waved the antique wellie at me. "Should be just about your size. Course, it's got holes and there was an old adder's nest in it, but it's better than going barefoot. Have it on the house."

So it was that I returned to the newsdesk, storyless, and with one foot encased in a boot that even the local snake population had condemned as unfit for habitation. Luckily for me, while I was out, the editor had discovered a story about a rottweiler with a conviction for gbh, that had been chased around a backyard by a pet rabbit. This made the front page, and in the excitement Editor Tel forgot all about the Calvi body. My adventure ended as an inside funny headline: *Footsore reporter gets the antique boot.*

You could understand, though, why for ten years after that, I had as little to do with the Thames Estuary as possible. Now, though, after all that time, that fruitless corpse-hunt came vividly to mind, as I first started to think about the Estuary in a deeply mature sort of way. That was when I remembered Skeet, too.

Skeet was one of those seemingly pointless memories, gathered as I'd plied my provincial hack's trade. Skeet had hung around unnoticed and unwanted, in some Salvation Army dosshouse for thoughts, in the back alleyways of the mind. Now I started to realise why he had kept his perch all these years.

It was summer and the silly season, so when the news editor learnt that a seagull needed a new home, she knew she might get home before midnight. "Ahhh, a lovely, cuddly little seagull, just what the doctor ordered," she said.

Skeet, the seagull in question, lived in the back-garden of a pigeon-fancier's house in Grays. The photographer and I found him there, doing his best to peck the eyes out of a concrete gnome.

"Unusual to find a seagull as a pet," I ventured.

"He's not a pet. He just set up home here without so much as a by-your-leave," said the pigeon-fancier. "He's a darn nuisance. He duffs up my pigeons. They keep coming last in their races because they don't want to fly back. Pigeons don't like violence you know, specially the domestic kind."

We went gingerly up to Skeet. The bird showed no fear, but no signs of friendship either. He spread his wings and gave vent to a complex sequence of hisses and squawks.

"If only birds could talk, eh," said the photographer.

"He can," said the pigeon fancier. "How much is that camera worth?"

"A lot of dosh," said the photographer.

"Right – well, he's advising you about a warm place where you can put it and nobody at all will want to steal it."

The foul-mouthed bird said something that was clearly even worse. Its involuntary master blushed.

"I don't think we can ask our readers to take that animal into their homes," I said. "Can't you just get the RSPCA to come and take it? They could release Skeet over the river. He'd be happy there."

"He came from the river in the first place," said the pigeon-fancier. "He was trying to get away from that sort of thing."

"What sort of thing?" I asked.

"Ask Skeet," said the pigeon-fancier. "He's got a tongue in his head hasn't he?"

I stuck the Sony tape-recorder carefully in front of Skeet's beak, half expecting him to bite it, or worse still, make racist remarks about the Japanese. But he reacted in an unexpected way. Instead of another aggressive squawk, he emitted a strange, high-pitched, ululating noise. It was a sound to break your heart.

"What's he saying?" the photographer asked.

"Well," said the fancier, "I'm not too strong on gull, dove is more my thing. But I think he's saying: 'The loneliness. The emptiness. The ...' – wait a sec, it's one of those long words. Just say it again Skeet."

The bird obliged.

"Desolation," said the fancier, "Is that an English word?"

The RSPCA never had to bother with Skeet in the end. He was found lying on his back with his legs stuck in the air some days later. Rat poison was suspected, though his injuries were consistent with having had a concrete gnome topple on him from a height.

Skeet was gone, but his melancholy vision lived on.

"The loneliness. The emptiness. The desolation," he had squawked.

Out on the Estuary, even the seagulls were lonely.

Trackless, uninhabited, and imbued with a melancholy that drove the very wildfowl to distraction, the Estuary was a scary place. After so many years, I finally realised something new about the mouth of the Thames.

Half a million people live within a mile of its shores. Its sea gateway is just thirty miles from the Houses of Parliament. Yet the Estuary is a wilderness. And while it may not be an exactly unexplored wilderness, it is something almost more desolate than its colleagues, like the Amazon or the Sahara. It is an unfashionable wilderness. Nobody, but nobody, takes an adventure holiday package there.

There was something else about it, too, something that made it almost unique in modern Britain. As that treasure-hunter had complained, there were no roads. To explore the shores of the great Thames Estuary, you have to walk.

Lonely marshland church – St Margaret, Bowers Gifford

Two

Blazed any good trails lately?

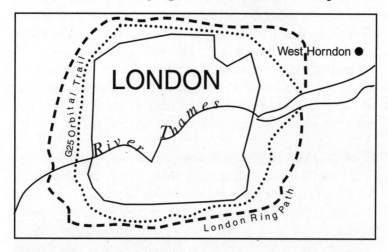

THE DOG and I have always been keen walkers. As an impoverished young journalist, I found that the hobby combined pleasant relaxation with a welcome boost to the income. All sorts of good things turned up on walks, including on one occasion a complete Marks & Spencer vest, still in its original packaging, in my size.

Living in Essex you do not – cannot – ramble in the same way as walkers from other counties. Other necks of the woods have downs, forests, heaths and country parks. A Chiltern or a Wales or two are always within easy striking distance, places where ramblers can stride freely all day, at least until their overheated pedometers need to be hosed down. Essex ramblers are quietly envious of this space and freedom to roam enjoyed by ramblers elsewhere. It is hard not to gloat when you hear of a backpacker scalped by a golden eagle or goosed by a Pennine peak. If you live in jam-packed suburbia, it is mildly satisfying to remember that there is a price to be paid for enjoying the wilderness.

My home countryside of south Essex has plenty of footpaths, alright, but they all tend to be about forty yards long. This represents the average length of a country path before the right of way is bisected by an obstacle. Such obstacles vary from natty commuter housing developments to stinking chicken broiler farms. Travellers' camps, quarries, lorry parks and supermarkets all add their bit to make a ramble challenging to the point of extinction. On one memorable occasion, I even found a swimming pool dug across the path. Around it lay three or four bikini-clad girls, accompanied by a millionaire, well-known to local reporters, and subsequently jailed for financial misdemeanours. As the little swimming party frolicked, thoughts of ramblers' rights were clearly not uppermost in their minds.

Above all, though, local footpaths are cut up by the roads so beloved of all Essex folk good and true. These roads range from the mighty M25 motorway, one of the greatest ramble-wrecking feats of all time, to odd strips of concrete in the middle of nowhere, constructed to siphon off some subsidy or other, or possibly just built for the sheer love of road-building. There is nothing that any walker can do about these obstacles, bar lie down in protest, which rather defeats the object of rambling.

A walker could sulk. A walker could take up an alternative pastime like counting the number of times the word MOO and COW appear on lorry registration plates. Or a walker could take a positive attitude, and decide that what can't be helped had better be enjoyed. This last was the approach taken by my children whenever our rambles were obliterated. Thus the concept of the Frustration Ramble, or Thwart-a-Walk, was born.

The rules of the Frustration Ramble are easily absorbed. Using an Ordnance Survey map, select two or three miles of official footpath. Set out along this path, score points for every obstacle, and see if you can beat your own previous record as you go along. Traditional rural obstacles such as an unbridged ditch, ploughed field, or an impossibly flatulent horse that causes a detour, score low (one point). A new house straddling the right of way does much better (five), unless the footpath has been diverted by proper procedures (three). A new road scores six. The best score ever was for an illicit farm reservoir. It had obliterated half the walk, so richly deserved its score of eight.

Occasionally, by way of contrast, we would walk in some other part of the world. We did the South-West peninsular path and Hadrian's Wall. Yet somehow, these well-marked, unobstructed trails were an anticlimax. Sixty miles of Pilgrims Way offered a lower frustration count than a good specimen of a blighted Essex path could offer in three miles, and sometimes with the added bonus of a burnt-out pub at the end of the route. The biggest disappointment of all was Snowdon. A ruddy great mountain, endless possibilities for taking a wrong turn or tumbling into a ditch – that ought to be worth at least fifty points. But no, the path ascended clear to the top, and there was an unclouded view from the summit. Pathetic! Score: Zero.

Then in the early 1990s, with little warning, the very survival of the frustration walk came under threat. The reason for this was the extraordinary spate of long-distance paths, heritage trails and council ambles that were unleashed upon the English countryside. In my own newspaper patch alone we acquired, in short order, an Essex Way, four town heritage trails, and, presumably for those on their last legs, a St Peter's Trail. There were also plans for a Yachtsman's Trail along the River Crouch, providing any dingy-sailor who had sunk in the river at least the consolation of a nice walk home to the yacht club.

At the time, the Lancashire rambler Alfred Wainwright had suddenly found himself one of the most famous people in the land, let alone on it. The shy fell-walker briefly became a fashion icon. Even in Essex, trendy youths could be observed with their trousers rolled up, muttering: "By gum, only twelve miles to ma' next sup o' ale lad." At least one domestic violence incident – always a good indicator of fashion trends – covered by the newsdesk involved the use of hiking boots as marital projectile weapons.

For a while, an entirely new class of frustration was added to our frustration walks. This took the shape of a chain-gang – well, chain-smoking anyway – composed of petty crimesters serving community service orders. The bad lads did a fine job. They cleared footpaths which had lain derelict for decades. They cut back vegetation. They removed fly-tips which they themselves had on some occasions been responsible for. They built foot-bridges. They built cattle-grids, the better to leg it the next time they ran away from a police-dog. They filled bogs with clinker, and – it was rumoured – at least one untidy picnicker who had messed up their work. A new class of punch-up was also added to the aggro-seeker's repertoire: the pruning-shears rumble.

In a true spirit of rehabilitation, I made every effort to absorb these gangs into the frustration system. A community service offender who stops to cadge a cigarette merits one frustration point. Being murdered by a footpath-clearer makes you the all-time frustration walk champion. Overall, though, the community service volunteers served to remove more frustrations than they created.

Meanwhile, the list of long-distance trails continued to burgeon. Plans were mooted for an Essex Pubs walk, a Will Kemp Way, a Three-Forests Walk. Serious-minded feminists proposed a Women Only trail, from which all rampant males would be banned except on open days.

As the home county maps filled up with trail names, attempts by would-be trailblazers to find new routes reached desperate proportions. They culminated in something quite extraordinary. At low tide, and around midnight, Shane Frome (not his real name), an unemployed pub-landlord, waded out across the Estuary mud. On shore, his estranged wife yelled curses at his figure as it disappeared into the gloom. But she made no attempt to warn the emergency services. An hour or so later, and with great good fortune, a fishing party discovered him stuck fast in the mud near the dredged channel. By dint of great ingenuity, the crew were able to dislodge him using their onboard winches. My newspaper reported the story, without names, stating merely that a middle-aged man had been rescued from the mudflats with little more than 45 minutes to spare before the waters covered him. The story ran to no more than three paragraphs. What set my nose twitching was the final paragraph. The man had told fishermen: "Leave me alone, I want to walk to Sheppey."

I'd known Mr Frome from his publican days. I now sought him out at home. Post-suicide attempt cold-calling is frowned on. Even hardened doorstepping reporters balk at questions like: "So why did you want to top yourself, pal?" or "So whereabouts did you *mean* to apply the chainsaw." However, I couldn't believe that Mr Frome would ever seek to kill himself. His self-regard was such that he would never want to deprive the world of his company or barbecuing skills. I found him at the top of the Southend high-rise where he lived. His considerable girth had been lowered into an armchair. A group of devoted children and ex-wives were tending to his needs. They had covered him with blankets, laid him on a sofa, and were using an electric fan-heater to warm the bits of his nether regions that had lain immersed in the mud.

"I've got a bone to pick with your newspaper," he growled at me as I came in. "Everyone's saying that I was trying to do myself in. Well, I wasn't, see."

"So what were you doing?"

"Walking across the Estuary, mate," he said, as if the answer was blindingly obvious to anybody except thick fishermen and journalists.

Shane's wife took me aside for a moment. "It is true," she said. "He was trying to top himself. I'd just told him I didn't love him any more, see. He couldn't take it."

"So he tried to drown himself?"

"He was wading out into the river so the tide would take away his misery. Is that sweet or what? I've never had anybody trying to kill themself for me before. He's a lovely man. I just love him so much."

This was just the sort of thing a desperate hack wanted to hear – 120-point front page headlines reading: *Marital tiff led to mud death bid* rolled across the Frome lounge. Then Shane spoilt it all.

"I don't know what she's been telling you," he said, "but I'll tell you how it was. I just wanted to get away from the cow. And suddenly the sea starts talking to me."

"What?"

"As I live and breathe. It says: 'Come on in, Shane, the water's lovely.' It was talking to me. Hissing like."

"'E was pissed," said his wife.

"No, I was stone cold, give or take a few jars. I'm telling you, I just wanted to walk across. I've always wanted to go to Sheppey," he said. Suddenly, amazingly, a tear rolled down his cheek. "It's not much to ask. Just a little old island," he grizzled. "Here, get me out of this."

A crack team of kids helped him off of his sofa, and heaved him toward the window. Much of the Estuary was visible from twelve storeys above Southend. Sheppey Island lay across the Estuary, a distant, grey, mysterious blur. "I see it every morning," intoned Mr Frome. "Been lots of places, I have. Been to Alaska, been to Gambia, been to Florida – sixteen times, actually. Been Majorca. But I never been to Sheppey. And you know something. Property prices are half what they are in Southend, a bloke told me. I'm sick of living in this dump. I used to own a house with four bedrooms on Benfleet Downs, before my little problems. So I looked at her" – he indicated his wife – "and I thought, I'm out of here. Never been to Sheppey, I'll just go over there now and get myself a nice little four-bedroom number and then I'll be in a decent place and I won't be looking across the Estuary at that stinking island any more because I'll be looking across the Estuary at stinking Southend instead."

I recognised his fascination for Sheppey Island. I shared it.

Sheppey is far away across the Estuary, it is usually shrouded with mist, it is covered with weird rectangular objects, and few people from Essex have ever been there and returned to tell the tale. Its sense of mystery makes it the nearest thing in the Estuary to an island of dreams, unless, that is, you happen to be on it. I had been on it.

Some years before, I had tried to assuage this sense of mystery. I set out to explore the periphery of Sheppey Island, walking along the coast opposite Southend. I headed east on the coastal path from Sheerness with high hopes. Within a mile or two of the town, however, the path had disappeared into a world of vast caravan parks. There were thousands of the things, stretching as far as the eye could see. These were the other-worldly rectangular objects, just visible from Southend using field-glasses.

I stumbled down the endless avenues of caravans. They all seemed to be identical, except for the flights of doorsteps, each of which took a pride in being distinctive and original. Many of these steps were made from recycled materials. At least one, I felt sure, had been put together from my great-aunt's casket, which I had last seen disappearing through a curtain in the Brentwood crematorium.

The caravan sites seemed to merge imperceptibly, but there must have been boundaries, because at regular intervals there were bad-tempered caretakers to be confronted. It was mid-week and early spring, and these caretakers were the only sign of human life. The first one emerged from a caravan, leaving behind a whirl of net-curtains.

"Can I help you, mate?" he asked, menacingly.

"Just taking a walk," I said.

"Walk?" he said incredulously. "Ain't you got no caravan?" he asked, with just a measure of pity for the hardships of the poor.

"No, I'm rambling," I explained.

"Rambling?" he said. "Rambling nutcase. You got some form of identification, then, to prove you're a rambler?"

The next caretaker, about half a mile further east, was set up in a caravan so splendid that at first sight it didn't look like a caravan at all. It looked more like the stately home that had been on the site before the caravan site was built. It was festooned with plasterwork Corinthian columns and statues. An old dog lay snoring in the front patch, oblivious to our approach.

"What you looking at mate," asked caretaker number two.

"Nothing," I said hurriedly. "I'll be on my way."

"Yes, you do that, or I'll get my dog to see you off," he said, unconvincingly. The dog gave a loud snore and stuck its nose further up its bottom, forming a near-perfect circle. It was hardly the most aggressive guard-dog posture. Even if it did snap its jaws, it would end up biting its own internals. However, the prospect of being pursued by a whirling doughnut with severe abdominal pain was alarming enough, and I made for the exit.

Caretaker number three started as the most aggressive of the bunch, if that was possible. He emerged snarling from a little prefab office building. He was clutching a copy of *Sporting Life*, held in both hands, levelled horizontally at me. I don't think he was doing it consciously, but I recognised his posture immediately as the Army Field Manual "Disembowel with fixed bayonet" stance. Okay, so the worst injury I could get from that rolled up paper would be a dodgy racing tip, and the fellow was 75 if he was a day. Yet there was something about his bearing that commanded a certain respect. I noticed too that my intelligent, cowardly dog had suddenly put a safe distance between us. This looked like a guy who had killed a few men in his time, possibly by rasping them with his stubble.

"Wha' you after then?"

"Just …"

"You're a ruddy traveller, aren't you. Want to steal my chickens, don't yer. Well, you can't, 'cos I've et 'em all, that's what

I've done."

"I'm not a traveller," I said.

"What are you then?"

I should have said "rambler" and left it at that. But it was not a term, or a concept, they seemed to recognise on Sheppey Island in those days. Very unwisely, I said: "A journalist."

The old man's eyes lit up. "A journalist, eh. Well, son, it's your lucky day. Have I got a story to tell you. Sorry about that welcome just then. We're all a bit careful, like, in these parts. Comes from the war, you know."

I knew the signs of a war story gathering.

"Well, sorry to bother you, we'll be on our way," I said.

"We was in the front line. You couldn't trust anybody – third columnists, you know. You saw a bloke you didn't recognise dressed as a vicar using a high-pitched voice, you told him to drop his trousers and put his hands up first. Mind you, not that I think a lot of these vicars needed any excuse to do that, if you know what I mean. Mind you, too, give me a good Hun on a parachute any day to some of the riffraff we get round here these days ..."

The story continued for what may well have been a couple of hours. He told a fantastical tale about how Winston Churchill had asked him in person to lie in a hidden bunker with a Tommy gun. After dark he had to emerge and harass any invading Germans. To his regret, no Germans had ever presented themselves for harassment. He had had to make do with caravan-owners ever since.

The sun waned, and with it waned all chances of walking any further. Eventually I headed back to Sheerness in a taxi with sore feet and ringing ears. Still, there was one good thing to be said for it. The failed circumnavigation of Sheppey possibly ranked as the all-time champion frustration walk.

So my memories of Sheppey Island consisted simply of countless caravans, guarded by suspicious, whiskery old gits. That was the reality. Yet from five miles across the Estuary, the caravans and the caretakers were invisible. They blurred into the soft purple haze of the mystery island.

Another reason why Sheppey is so mysterious is that nobody ever goes there. People live there, but they don't go there. There are islands that people go to, like Hawaii, but Sheppey isn't one of them. Sheppey, however, does have one thing in common with Hawaii – it takes a long time to get there. To arrive on wheels the traveller must take the rackety branch-line railway or the slow, low road across the marshes. The weary traveller is then confronted by Tesco and a clock tower, so not surprisingly most pleasure-seekers with a car or train at their disposal prefer to head on south-east to the Whisky A-Go-Go club in Paris instead. Even Sheppey residents tend to prefer that. The Whisky-A-Go-Go club is full of them.

Sheppey is a very lonely place. Southend and Sheerness, the capital of Sheppey, are like relatives who haven't spoken to each other for a very long time. They have confronted one another across the Estuary since the dawn of time, without ever achieving much communication. Probably there was more contact in the days when Southend brontosauruses bellowed to Sheerness frumposauruses across the primeval swamps.

I know all this for a fact thanks to a quick vox pop. Standing on Southend's Pier Hill, I asked a random sampling of fourteen adults the simple question: "Have you ever been to Sheppey island." Three had been there, eight said they had never set foot on the place, and three said: "Where's Sheppey?", even though they were looking at it.

For just a few years, it is true, Southend and Sheppey were physically linked. During World War II, a barrier stretched across the Estuary mouth, linking the two places. The intention was to keep out enemy E-boats, submarines, and the odd clue-less Nazi day-tripper. In the event, the E-boats never came. In place of hostile action, and to while away cold nights on the barrier, a fierce macho rivalry developed between Kent and Southend defence crews, as they vied with one another to see who could produce the fattest and longest roll-up cigarette.

After the war, the councils on both sides wasted no time in demolishing the barrier, giving this priority even over the provision of council milk to children. Since 1946, Southend and Sheerness, the two Estuary gateway towns, have resumed their age-old posture of cold defiance to one another. To underline the point, Southend Pier points directly at Sheerness in a manner that some would deem outright rude.

Yet now, all of a sudden, everyone wanted to go to Sheppey, even if they felt they had to walk across the Estuary to do so. A short time after Shane Frome had attempted his cross-Estuary hike, a teenage burglar, pursued on foot by the police, dived into the water, still wearing the jeans he had just filched from Man About Town. The Southend high-speed inflatable lifeboat was called out to rescue him. Coxswain Paul Gilson discovered the lad, floundering in surf, several hundred feet offshore. He was hauled into the boat by the scruff of his neck. "Just what do you think you are up to, son?" asked Gilson. "Just going to visit me cousins in Kent. I got a right to, ain't I," said the lad.

There was also the matter of the Estuary Barrage. This was a project for a vast dam, to be built from Southend to Sheppey. Its ostensible purpose was to replace the Woolwich Barrage when that great structure wore out and retired to some nice up-country fishing pond. However, I noticed that the report contained the tell-tale phrase "To include a footpath on the top for rambling and cycling leisure pursuits." Someone was trying to create a multi-billion pound hiking trail by stealth.

So a pattern was emerging of attempts, many desperate, to create a cross-Estuary path. I was already spending a lot of time watching the Thames, and I now began to look out for any Sheppeyites who might be attempting to return the compliment and splash across in the other direction. The desperate, atavistic need in human beings to blaze a footpath somewhere should never be underrated.

Back on dry land, someone managed the unthinkable, and came up with a brand new idea for a long-distance path. The newsdesk on the *Evening Bellow* received a press release announcing the birth of the G25. This was to be an orbital footpath system, allowing ramblers to circumnavigate London without even once getting themselves squashed by a 44-ton truck. The G stood for Green, and the 25 was an echo of the M25 motorway that carried traffic more noisily, but usually rather more slowly, round the capital.

The G25 cut a thin little swathe through Essex north from the river and through the Belton hills at Thorndon Park. It was here that a very important hiking bigwig was to visit the volunteers who were busy erecting sign-posts and fixing footbridges on the G25. The local press was invited to pay court on the Saturday in question. "Here's one for the anorak desk," said the news editor, passing me the press-release.

A few days later, another press-release about the London orbital pathway arrived. Something odd had happened. The G25 had now changed its name to the London Ring Path, and the route had changed completely, moving two miles to the east. However, the press were still welcome to visit the pioneers on any Saturday.

The photographer and I duly turned up at this new site, to find a group of pioneers in designer scrub-bashing gear. They were presided over by a pleasant retired schoolmaster.

"I've come to cover the official visit by Alan Monday," I told him.

The effect on the old man was quite startling.

"Alan Monday! Alan Monday himself! Gracious me, nobody informed us of this. I'd have worn a respectable anorak if I'd known that the great man was coming to view our little scheme."

I checked the press release. The date and details seemed okay. "This is the G25, isn't it?" I said.

"No, I don't believe there is such a thing as the G25," said the schoolmaster. "I believe that you may be confusing it with the M25, a motor road that rings our capital city. We are in the process of creating the London Orbital Ring, which is intended to be a pleasant trackway for pedestrians alone. We rather liked the word 'ring'. It has a certain Tolkienish or Wagnerian smack of high adventure to it, does it not?"

Looking at what the working party has achieved, I began to see his point. They had made quite a splash on the landscape. The route crossed country, using old footpath routes, but in a blaze of new stiles, fingerposts and footbridges. Nettle patches were being thwacked, unsuspecting brambles ambushed. Fifteen or twenty good frustration points were disappearing in front of my eyes, and something newly created was taking their place.

"So what's in it for you, mate?" asked the photographer.

"I suppose the answer to your question would be: a measure of immortality," said the schoolmaster. "Every time a rambler sets grateful foot upon this pathway, he will in effect be placing a posy of flowers upon my grave."

He may have been retired, but he was a darn good teacher, I'll say that. His message struck home. A trackway! What a way to be famous. What a way to be remembered. I imagined a route called the Old Tomway, snaking through the land. Hundreds of years from now, exhausted walkers would flop down beside the path and ask old Tom, who he? "Some grim old tribal chieftain with three thousand children who used the track to get from one wife to another, no doubt," one would say.

His companion would put him right. "No, no. He was a local hack from these parts. He hacked for the newspaper and he hacked the local vegetation." And they would shudder delightfully at the thought of such a wild, primitive creature, and pat their blisters with methylated spirits as a way of paying appropriate tribute.

At this time in life, words like "immortality" and "everlasting" were starting to have a strange, Pavlovian effect on me.

Someone only had to mention them and various bits at the sharp end of the anatomy would go into panic mode. My knee-joints would stiffen, my back would creak, and I would instinctively run my tongue round my teeth to ensure that they were all still hanging in there.

Along with a sense of the brevity of life went an increasing urge to leave something tangible behind. But what monument could I offer? A pile of cuttings covering over 3,000 horticultural shows wasn't much of a legacy, and anyway, I was trying to give up flower-shows, since all that talk about "perennials" had a devastating effect on my physique.

However, there was no time to dream of such things. We had an important footpath official to locate. The photographer and I next made our way to West Horndon where the great man was due to arrive by train. We found another group of ramblers with pickaxes waiting to greet him.

"I guess you're the Ringway people ,"I said

"We call it the G25," said chief rambler. And it was at this point that I twigged. There were two different groups, both hacking pathways round London, and both seemingly unaware of one another's existence. Here was high old sport to be sure.

· The train drew up at this point and out stepped the great Al Monday. The reverence with which he was treated just had to be seen to be believed. Chief rambler called him "guvnor". One rambler pulled a comb out of some recess in his rucksack and ran it through his hair, in what I took to be a modern version of doffing the forelock.

The ramblers then set off from the station on a two-mile walk to a showpiece section of the orbitway, where a picnic buffet awaited them. The photographer and I took the long, unhealthy route round in our smog-puffing cars. Two miles nearer London we found a second trail, barely out of sight of the first one we had visited. Here we found yet more ramblers gathered on G25, eagerly awaiting the arrival of the great chief. The trestle table had been spread with a sort of long-distance hiker's cuisine, including some reconstituted curries designed to be mixed with ditchwater, a gateau made from Kendal mint-cake, and thin slices of dehydrated buffalo that someone had brought back as a souvenir from the forests of North America.

The rambling bigwigs arrived from the railway station at sur-prising speed, hurtling along the new trackway, preceded by a terrified stampede of snails and grass-snakes. I briefly inter-viewed Al Monday about his illustrious walking career – most-ly spent pacing ministerial corridors in Whitehall – and his hopes for the G25. Then, right at the end, I slipped in a men-tion of the other new trackway.

"How do you react to the fact that, at this moment in time, a rival pathway around London is being implemented by a sep-arately designated organisation. Is this not a misallocation of scarce resources at a time of severe cutbacks in basic source funding?" I enquired, in language that Mr Monday would understand.

"It's news to me, this other project," he said. "Still, it sounds like an amateur effort. I'm sure they'll soon give up. I don't think we need trouble ourselves further with them, do you?"

"No, sir," I answered, and then realised what I had said. I'd called him sir. When had I last called anybody "sir"? Nobody uses the word sir in Essex. Deference is an unknown quality. We don't even show deference to the Queen. When Her Majesty opened Stansted Airport in 1992, the musical compere and former newsreader Richard Baker introduced the proceedings. I listened as three pressmen greeted him with a royal fanfare they had been practising for the occasion, achieved by breaking wind in three-part harmony. Then, halfway through the speech by the Queen herself, a drunken photographer had toppled off the press-stand into a pile of camera bags and Parka anoraks, where he lay, peacefully snoring. No, veneration and sub-servience were definitely extinct qualities where I came from.

Yet here we all were, bowing and scraping to a man for no better reason than he had acquired a spot of gold braid on his rucksack. I noted how the ranks of ramblers parted as he made his way to the buffet table. I noted how they politely waited until Mr Monday himself had started to eat, first checking his buffalo "jerky" (dried meat) for accidentally dehydrated udders, before they partook. I knew that Alfred Wainwright was subject to similar veneration. The message was clear. In 1990s England, the path to glory was just that – the path. Don't be a politician, film-director or captain of industry, my son, be a rambling man.

Despite his assumed nonchalance about the rival working-party up the road, I noticed that Mr Monday had an urgent word or two with some of the scrub-bashers, complete with a circular cupping of his hands gesture, which might have signi-fied a footpath surrounding London, or might have signified the strangling of the rival footpath-makers, though as humanely as possible, of course.

Quite soon the pioneers laid down their sandwiches and picked up their pruners. The race was on.

I spent the next few weeks in a state of deep brooding. Build a trail – that was the key to fame and immortality. Yet where from and to, and why, and did you offer Air Miles with it? Even in the course of these few weeks, others more resourceful than I were building their own trails. A Thundersley Downs trail opened up, and a Dick Turpin trail, which promptly had some of its signposts nicked by some sort of modern highwaymen. Soon every footpath in southern England would have become part of someone or other's trail, and the golden ego-trip oppor-tunity would be lost forever.

One winter's afternoon, while we waited to pick up my daughter from a ballet class, the dog and I took a walk along the cliff-tops at Leigh-on-Sea. And brooded. And brooded some more. The greensward that runs along the Leigh heights is a good place to contemplate mortality. It is packed with the eld-erly, gamely taking the sea air and a few inches of exercise. They say you are becoming old when the police constables first start to look young. A lady in a bright silk headscarf shuffled past. "She looks a bit young to be using a Zimmer frame," I said to the dog. Then the full implication of what I had said hit me.

"Oh God," I told the dog. "I'm getting older. My bones are starting to ache and I'm showing classic signs of senile decay. I'm unburdening myself to a dog, for heaven's sake. In a few years from now, I'm going to be lying in a grave on Downham hilltop. Worms will eat my best features and the rest will wash downhill to the Estuary. From there I will be washed out to sea, evaporated, rained onto the earth. For millions of years I will filter down through limestone strata. One billion years from now I will pop up in somebody's bottle of pure, natural mineral water and that will be all there is to show for ever having been here."

Essex Dog, however, was too preoccupied with her walk and with investigating passing pensioners' elasticated stockings to pay much attention to my cosmic whingeing. Essex Dog wasn't worried about immortality. A good walk in the here and now was all that mattered to her, cosmically speaking.

The dog's presence was infectious, thanks to her attitude to life as well as her fleas. The pleasure of walking and the evening beauty of the grey old Estuary soon knocked the blues away. I got to thinking once again about long distance paths. And I remembered William Waight. In 1791, Will was buried in Hockley churchyard, about four miles to the north of the Estuary. He lies, at his own request, just outside the porch-door. So everyone who goes to church walks over his gravestone. Will left firm instructions in his will that this was the spot where he wanted to be buried. "People have trampled all over me in life, so they might as well do so in death as well," he declared, sourly. Yet the fact is that people remember Will, and they don't remember the people who did the trampling.

"Get people to walk all over your memory. That's the key to immortality," I told the dog.

But where, where, in this over-peopled, over-walked island was there such a thing as an untrodden trackway?

At this point, the entire Thames Estuary turned from grey to blue, then gathered all its waters into a great big eye-shaped puddle, and winked at me. Then it blew a huge saltwater raspberry, and reverted to grey, inert evening shadows.

However, like everybody else walking or living on the lower Thames's banks that evening, I was studiously ignoring the Estuary, and failed to notice the fact that it was trying to tell me something blindingly obvious.

The sight must have registered at the back of my brain, though. Months later, that rude, leering river jostled its way into a dream. I woke up, in the early hours, in a lather of excitement.

"That's it," I said to my wife. "That's the walk to do!"

My wife slept on, unmoved. So I made my way downstairs to the kitchen, where another unresponsive female, Essex Dog, lay with her legs stuck rigid in the air, snoring with surprising volume.

"I've got it," I told her. "An Estuary Trail." The dog snored on.

I poured a glass of water – good Thames water, albeit with a bit of silver paint added by the water-company to disguise the mud colour. I raised it in a toast before drinking it.

"Here's to the estuary walk," I said. "What a great idea."

Contained in that tumbler, the estuary looked a meek enough undertaking. "Can't think why nobody's walked round you before," I told the glass of water.

I was soon to find out just why.

Laurence Watts (left) and John Skinner, Essex naturalists, at Southend Pier

Idealised version of the Thames Estuary – The Bluewater Canal

Three

Foulness – Mystery Island

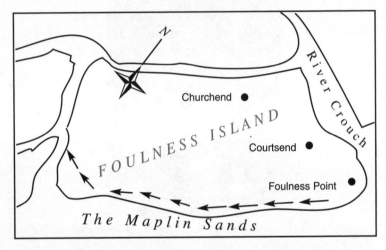

ON A BRIGHT morning Essex Dog and I mounted the sea-wall at Foulness Point, and began to walk round the shores of the Thames Estuary.

The choice of Foulness as starting point had only been arrived at after a lot of consideration and the wearing out of several maps – though perhaps I should have just purchased a decent Ordnance Survey sheet to start with, rather than trying to use the free ones on the back of the bus timetable.

Technically, the north shore of the Thames Estuary begins and ends at Shoebury Ness. The land, in the shape of Foulness Island, then turns away to the north-east. But no place better embodies the spirit of the Thames Estuary than this lonely island. The name supposedly comes from the wildfowl who inhabit it, not least a colony of feral parrots noted for their dirty laughs. Many authorities on place names, however, quietly harbour a different conviction. Could Foulness have been named for the foul language that it provoked from its inhabitants. The great sea-fogs would roll in from the Maplin Sands. In the white silence, you could hear a pin drop, and sailors marooned a mile or more away would hear the farmers cursing. They knew what this meant. The poor sod-busters were trying to persuade their oxen to plough a straight furrow, although they couldn't see so much as a yard in front of their hooves in the fog. And the heartfelt words: "How am I supposed to farm this *******　place?" would drift out to sea.

The basic facts on Foulness are these: the island is roughly five miles long, and two and a half miles wide. It is bounded by the open sea to the east, the River Crouch estuary (yes, another of those things) to the north, the River Roach to the west and a tidal creek, the Middleway, to the south. It has a tiny, resident farming population of about 250. Youngsters tend to move away – Foulness, as an address, has just about the least street cred in Britain, owing to there not being any streets.

Apart from its wildfowl, Foulness has been noted since before the Norman Conquest for boasting some of the best farmland in Essex, for those freezing sea-fogs that blanketed it, and for being, even by the standards of lonely, wandering Saxon seafarers, a remote Hicksville of a place.

In the years before the World War I a new sort of fog descended on Foulness Island – the fog of secrecy. The War Department gradually acquired holdings on the island, and in 1915 it bought the ancient Lordship of the Manor of Foulness, after the death of the last squire, Alan Finch.

Foulness promptly turned into Hush-Hush Island – a place of weird gadgetry, strange science-fiction noises, grim rumours and cosmically significant secrets, its perimeters constantly patrolled by huge wolf-dogs with the grim dedication of bouncers at a first-list Hollywood wedding-party. Once upon a time Foulness was the island that nobody wanted to go to. Now it became the island that nobody could get onto, now that they finally did want to.

Whatever happens on the island, it employs a lot of local

people. Local journalists get used to a certain response to the question: what do you do for a living? "Oh, I work with the MOD on F...f...f..." and the quick change of subject: "Er, would you like a cup of tea? One lump of nuclear Armageddon, I mean sugar, or two?"

A gatehouse now blocks the one and only road onto the island, and a high-wire fence that would administer a mid-air gelding to even the most soaring Soviet bloc pole-vaulter, surrounds the perimeter. Thus, ultra-secretive, sinister and still mist-shrouded (all that hi-tech military technology didn't seem able to do much for the island's weather), Foulness maintains its role as a real-life James Bond location – minus, of course, the bikini-clad girls, who would freeze to death in no time.

In March 1969 the bodies of three duck-hunters were found just off the island, and steam started to hiss out of the valves of the rumour mills. The official story was that the wildfowlers had simply lost their way in the fog. Gentlemen and ladies of the press began to be waylaid by nervy individuals with hats or toupees pulled down over their eyes. These eyeless ones had a different story to tell – of shots ringing out in the mist, of a Russian ship moored off the island at dead of night, and of something called the "Speznatz".

The Speznatz were supposedly a crack team of Russian behind-the-lines commandos, and they were so secretive that they made Foulness look like the Cilla Black Christmas show. In the event of a Russian communist invasion, it would be the Speznatzis' job to disguise themselves as milkmen, bowler-hatted City businessmen, and other inconspicuous types. They would then blow up bridges, cut power-lines, and assassinate important local dignitaries, such as the mayor and possibly the chief milkman.

While the enslaved workers of Essex awaited this liberation, the Speznatz undertook a sort of sophisticated reconnaissance role, spying on places such as GCHQ in Cheltenham, and, inevitably, Foulness Island. The belief in many quarters was that the deceased wildfowlers had stumbled on a group of Speznatzi.

Just what were the Speznatzi so interested in? Extraordinary rumours began to circulate about the island. It was said to be the storehouse for Old Kickarse, the most powerful nuclear bomb in the world, mighty enough to take out several US states in one go, and stored here in England because an accident back home might have negatively influenced too many American voters. The Ministry of Defence had agreed to take the bomb, the story continued, on one condition. Two minutes before the end of the world, we should be allowed to drop it on the French.

UFO watchers had a different theory. The Estuary has an enormous number of UFO watchers, and several clubs devoted to the pleasant pastime of observing little green men the way other enthusiasts observe newts. The UFO watchers will tell you that this is because the Estuary has the highest concentration of alien visitations of anywhere except Salisbury Plain. Their explanation for Foulness goes like this: any alien unlucky enough to be captured by the local constabulary is escorted to the island for internment and interrogation. The place is now crawling with grounded aliens. Just why these aliens should choose to voyage through countless eons of time and space in order to land in the Thames mud, when they could just as easily visit Disneyworld, is one of the mysteries of the universe. Maybe it's just to visit all those relatives on Foulness.

All this was just part of the sinister, enigmatic mythology that surrounded Foulness Island. Yet on this sunny morning, Foulness didn't look in the least bit sinister or enigmatic. At first sight, the place was a great disappointment. Just neat fields, a spattering of houses and barns, and great East Anglian skies. Then we reached the top of the sea-wall – and gasped, and stared. Nothing quite prepares you for your first sight of the Maplin Sands.

The sands stretch to the horizon, and even at high tide, the sea is only a shallow covering. The noise made by the waves is like nothing else on the seven seas, a sort of irregular rasping noise, reminiscent of a spade being dragged along a concrete path by someone with terminal hiccups. Yet the most astonishing thing about the Maplins was their sheer emptiness. There were no ships or boats, not so much as the usual unhinged windsurfer normally to be found in such places, to be seen. There were just these level sands, stretching away for ever, or at least until the curvature of the earth put an end to their flatness.

There is a technical reason for this emptiness. Ancient mariners refer to it as being blown to gobspray. Since the early nineteenth century, big guns of every description have been blasting the sands. Throughout that time, the Maplins have been the testing ground for everything British with a big barrel and a bad attitude. Naval guns, field guns, guns too big of girth to do anything except stay put in Shoeburyness, have all launched rounds of high explosive onto those long-suffering quicksands. Millions of tons of unwanted munitions have also been destroyed here. The funny thing is, after being blown up for almost two centuries in the cause of military science, the Maplins still look exactly as they did before guns were invented. It also seems strange that, though the boom of the big guns of Shoebury can be heard in London, the effect of the Maplins is of an uncanny stillness.

From the sea-wall there was also a good view of the island itself. There was not much more sign of life here, either. Just huge, well-kept fields and, on the far side of the island, some giant hangers, clearly designed to house flying-saucers, or possibly to hang out soggy combat fatigues on Foulness's many wet days. The army road was also visible, bisecting the island. It led to the island's two tiny villages, just visible through trees on the north of the island, Churchend and Courtsend. In the past, the inhabitants of the two villages regarded people from the neighbouring village with deep suspicion, although they were less than one mile apart. Once a year the two cricket teams grudgingly played against each other. For the rest of the year the Foulness villages ignored the "furriners" from the next village, although isolated together in the middle of a wilderness.

The island was as silent as the sands. The only sign of life was a tractor in the far distance, painstakingly working one of those enormous fields. Apart from that, it was a world devoid of humanity. The fact that, a few feet underground, hundreds of aliens were being grilled by intelligence officers with lisps from minor public schools, had no effect on the landscape itself.

Or had the world just ended? That was it. The rest of England had perished in a giant explosion, but Foulness was protected by some star wars invisible shield. Armageddon had arrived, and, as with all really good news stories, I'd been some-where else.

And so, all alone, the dog and I, the last ramblers left alive, took the first tentative steps of the Great Estuary Walk.

We were on top of the great concrete dyke that is Essex's answer to the Great Wall of China. It may not be so long or so tall, but it gives the Chinese version a good run for its money when it comes to the number of discarded pot-noodle packets along the way. In one guise or another, this sea-wall snakes along the entire length of the Essex coast, except for Purfleet, where there is a freak cliff. Without the wall, about one fifth of Essex would disappear underwater at regular intervals in the winter, and usually, no doubt, just when families everywhere were planning a picnic.

In one or two places, a medieval clay dyke still does the job. For the most part, though, the sea-wall is a prosaic concrete embankment, scoured white by the sea-spray and the wind. About half a billion pounds worth of reinforced concrete makes for a comfortable, if rather expensive, footpath.

And it was ours, all ours. We were in the grip of that sense of sheer, fantastic exhilaration that always sets in at the start of a long distance walk, before leaking boots and rising damp of the spine begin to sodden the spirits. Alright, so this wasn't

such a long walk; at the end of the day I was going to drive back
to wife and children, and I was walking through a landscape I'd
been staring at all my life. Still, it really was the start of – a
cliché I'd been dying to use all my life – the journey of a lifetime.

The first hour passed without much change in the scenery.
We might have been doing punishment drill, marching up and
down on the spot, for all the difference. Essex Dog, easily bored,
began to whine. Her body language, always deeply expressive,
registered the words: Can we do the Pennine Way instead? I
was pondering a reply when at last, we arrived at something
interesting, and obviously top secret. There was a ..., and a tall
..., and a bizarre ..., and a huge, lowering. ... Alas, I'd promised not to write about any of them.

One of the best kept of all Foulness secrets is this: it is actually
quite easy to get onto the island. It needn't be a secretive operation. A frogman's outfit is not necessarily required (especially
by ramblers, who look silly walking in them). All you need to
do is write to Comax, the organisation that administers security for the ranges, on behalf of the Ministry of Defence. This I
did, and in due course received my marching orders.

They were very specific. I had to keep strictly to the sea-
wall, not straying so much as one yard off the path. The walk
had to be undertaken on a Friday afternoon or at weekends,
when the big guns were silent and there was no chance of spoil-
ing government high explosive shells. Binoculars and cameras
were forbidden. So were "optical instruments", though why
anybody imagined that I might want to test my eyes in the middle of a walk was beyond me. I could report on birds, bees, per-
sonal emotions, the landscape, the weather and the state of my
feet. I should not write about any structure that had "Property
of MI5" stencilled on it, or any normally inanimate object like,
say, a deckchair, that had eyes, or antennae, or both. I should
not give any descriptions or the whereabouts of buildings,

should I happen to find any, or for that matter, fall into one. And I wasn't to say anything at all, let alone "Hi sailor!", to any military personnel I might encounter. These restrictions excepted, the freedom of Foulness was ours.

All these stipulations I agreed to. Yet I still had a secret mission. I might look like a local hack in a dirty rucksack. In reality, I was a secret agent. I was working for an organisation so secretive that it didn't have a name. But this organisation meant business. Its aim was nothing less than to peel back the most hidden of all the secrets on Mystery Island.

For the sake of this text, they will be referred to as FUM – the Foulness Underground Movement. FUM had operated as an underground cell for some years, but in 1989 one of their number broke cover long enough to accost me, as a representative of the local media, with a request.

FUM-1, as we shall call him, chose his venue carefully. It was the Southend Annual Model Railway exhibition. I was there, but reluctantly. Scale model railways weren't really my scene. Also, I'd never quite got over the shock of accidentally crunching a complete carriage-load of commuters underfoot in a friend's toy-room when I was young. However, a sadistic editor had dispatched me to do a story on the exhibition. He had already written the sarcastic headline: "The one railway system that really works." I had to write the piece to go with the headline.

The exhibition was a grave disappointment, storywise. There were no train-wrecks, drunkard signalmen, or miniature figures of virginal ladies tied to the railway lines. Mostly the modellers had created alpine railway systems, and, for some reason, lots of scale-model warehouses. There was, however, one system that stood out. It was a very sinister little model railway, though it was hard to work out exactly why. The setting was indeterminate, though it could well have been some Iron Curtain country. As usual, there were lots of warehouses, but they were very run down. And they were protected by lots of miniature barbed-wire. There were hammers and sickles all over the place, even on the loo doors. On the ground there was a smattering of what was obviously meant to be snow, though the modeller hadn't quite got it right. It looked like toothpaste accidentally left behind in the wash-basin. Oddest of all, many of the little human figures in the display wore dark glasses, despite the freezing temperatures and minus thirty degrees toothpaste.

Standing next to the display, almost as inert as the plastic models, and also wearing dark-glasses, was a man I vaguely knew, though not by name. He worked in the graphics business, and stuck posters of railway engines above his desk. In similar places on the wall, his colleagues posted pictures of Busty Bertha, the page three girl with an interest in ecological psychology.

Without so much as a how d'ye do, he said: "I've got a bit of investigative journalism for you, Mr King."

All newspapermen hear this intro-line a lot, and it's often the prelude to a plea for help from someone who's lost their cat. But I paid more attention when the dark train-buff continued: "You can get a pass onto Foulness Island, can't you?"

"Possibly. Why?"

He glanced around, nervously. "Shhh," he said. "You never know who might be listening. They plant bugs everywhere. Talk to me over the lay-out. It's the one place that's safe from spies." He indicated the Stalinist terror railway track, with its dozen or more plastic secret agents.

I bent over the model lay-out and he leaned over from the other side. With our noses resting on either end of the Communist pedestrian railway bridge, he told his tale.

"What do you know about the Foulness Underground?"

"Never heard of them. What are they supposed to be rebelling against."

"No, no, the Underground train. Like in London Underground."

A Foulness Underground! I realised now that my friend was

terminally loopy. I had to humour him, or he might attack me. I vaguely looked around for a makeshift defensive weapon. He understood railway regulations. If I waved a red model signal-lamp at him, perhaps that would stop him in his tracks.

"It doesn't sound likely," I said. "I mean, you're the expert and all that, but I thought undergrounds were for big cities. Foulness is about the emptiest place in England."

"You think that Foulness is just wild birds and seals?" said FUM-1. "That island has a complete Underground train system, just like the Circle Line only better, and we want to get our hands on it."

"We?"

"We're a splinter group from the Train Society. Even the other members don't know about us. You know what a cell is? We're one of them things. But it's very dangerous. I'm telling you, two of our members have already been killed by the Secret Service."

I stared at FUM-1. Irritation at having all this time wasted by a conspiracy theorist was starting to obtain the better of tact. "Do you honestly expect me to believe all this? There's only one road on the island. Why should they need an Underground system?"

"I'm telling you, Mr King, it's a treasure railway, that Foulness Underground," said FUM-1, totally ignoring my remark. "All the old rolling-stock since Edwardian times has gone there. You think all those Underground carriages going down the Arterial Road are headed for the breaker's yard on Shoebury, don't you? That's what they tell you. But I'm telling you, mate, the carriages don't get broken up, they go straight onto the rails on that Underground railway on the island."

This brought me up short for a moment. The sight of Underground carriages making their way down the A127 London-Southend road on the back of a low-loader, or even more bizarrely, parked on the forecourt of the Blinking Owl café, is one of the more rum sights of Estuary-land. But he was right, in this respect at least. Nobody ever sees or hears anything more about them. It's as if they disappear into a hole in the ground ...

At this stage we had to stop our conversation. Our conspiratorial huddle was producing the opposite effect to what was intended. People were gathering round FUM-1's model railway in the hope of finding just what it was we didn't want them to hear. "We'll contact you," he hissed. "Now slip into the crowd. If *they* get wind of this, you'll go the same way as Ray and Roy." He made a noise which I assumed to be a gun-silencer, spitting straight into my face in the process.

As it happened, three years were to pass before I encountered FUM again. A thousand stories came and went, and then one day I received, in the mail, a square of paper, folded many times, enclosed in a thick manila envelope. It invited me to meet up for a drink in the Bullseye pub in Basildon. The writer promised he could put me onto a scandal. He didn't identify himself, but he said he would recognise me from my mugshot in the paper.

At the Bullseye, I was soon approached by a nervy trio of middle-aged men. They were the unhealthiest-looking bunch you could imagine. They insisted on sitting in a dark corner of the pub.

"It's about the Underground," said one.

"Oh, right. The one on Foulness." This time there was no confusion. Memories of that strange encounter at the model railway exhibition came flooding back, with near total recall.

"No, not on, *under* Foulness," said one of the group, pedantically.

"I talked about it at the model railway exhibition. Tall bloke, worked in graphics, don't know his name. One of you lot, was he?"

"That's George," said a FUM man. "I'm sorry to say he's dead now."

"What!" He wasn't very old."

"To tell you the truth, we reckon it was the Secret Service that got to him. We keep losing members that way, it's a crying shame."

"I don't recall any shootings on this patch in recent years," I said.

"No, no. It was made to look like a heart attack. They're really good at covering up their tracks, those people."

"It's bad, you know," said another FUM. "You go into railways to escape the stresses of life and you end up dead, and more stressed out than ever."

Looking at this group of railway conspiracy theorists, it was easy to imagine them being picked out for early promotion by the Grim Reaper. But it had nothing to do with any assassin. One of them had actually managed to acquire a pork pie, an object I hadn't seen for years. He was guzzling it as we talked. I was fascinated by the thought of their joint cholesterol count – it was no wonder that they kept keeling over and dying. So fascinated, indeed, that I could barely pay attention when they started to talk in earnest about the Underground railway.

"We're worried about that railway …

"All this business with Glasnost and the end of the Cold War and the Berlin Wall coming down and things …"

"They're going to close down Foulness. They just don't need all that secret stuff there any more."

"But what's going to happen to that Underground railway? That's what we need to know. If we don't do something about it, they may fill it in – or just let the sea get into the system."

"Hold on," I said. "Even supposing there is such a thing as a Foulness fast Tube service, why does it matter what happens to it?"

"Because," said a FUM, "we want it. Nowhere in the world is there a tube-train system run by amateurs. Think what it would be like as a tourist attraction. 'A journey in darkness through the heart of the Estuary slime.' And think of all that old rolling-stock. They'd come from all over the world for the experience. Eat your heart out Bluebell Railway."

The argument had a certain compulsion. But I couldn't understand where I came in. The FUMs wasted no time in explaining.

"It's no good us going to the perimeter guard station on Foulness and saying we want to save the Underground. They'd shoot us. Or, worse still, they'd laugh at us and call us trainspotters."

"But if you write about it in the paper, better still start a campaign – that will have an effect."

"But I'm not even convinced there is an Underground train on Foulness," I told them. To myself I thought: "if I start babbling about it on the newsdesk they'll reckon I need a therapeutic rest and put me on the children's letters page."

"Go on the island and see for yourself."

"How can I? Even if I can get a pass, the Underground's under ground."

At this point, the encounter became truly weird. "Just look," said one of the FUMs, "for signs of the silver leaf."

"Er, what?"

"You'll see rows of them above the railway. There's no plant like them anywhere else. They're like sort of bits of Christmas tinsel on sticks. They grow where the ground's been disturbed when they dug the railway."

If I remember right, I terminated the conversation there and then. Seven more years passed, and I gave little thought to Undergrounds of any description.

And now, here I was, walking the length of Foulness and casing the lonely island for hot news. It was then that I remembered, with some gratitude, the Foulness Underground Movement.

Scenery is all very well, and Foulness has plenty of it. But you can't actually do anything with scenery except perhaps paint it, build all over it or run a rave concert on it – and darn it, I'd left the rock band at home. Added to which, the mudflats of the Essex coast don't really change from one league to the next. After two hours of tramping and no shipwrecks, no human beings to pounce on for an impromptu interview, and no hope whatever of a decent road traffic accident, I was becoming a mite restless. Added to which, the clear, steady course of the sea-wall provided perfect walking. Result: frustration count: Zero.

I also realised that, once the first exhilaration of the walk had subsided, a strange depression was setting in. At first I put it down to the vast, soul-crushing bleakness of the Maplin Sands. Then the thought struck that the Army might be practising some sort of invisible psychological warfare. It made sense. An invading army of Speznatzi storms ashore. Then they're hit by a closely targeted barrage of clinical depression. They promptly burst into tears, and sit down to write letters to their mums. Or call their psychotherapy battalion sergeants on their mobile phones. It would fit in with the modern, caring way of doing warfare.

Once I started Underground spotting, however, tedium and depression both evaporated. Every stunted tree or pile of old tyres became a potential Bond Street tube entrance. I even found myself looking out for signs of the famous red circular London Transport logo.

I tried to recall details of the conversation with the FUMs. Somehow, in the strange atmosphere of Foulness Island, their ideas seemed a lot less weird. Could their various theories help to identify the whereabouts of the railway? FUM had two basic conspiracy theories to explain the presence of this railway. Theory number one, the most convincing, was the Armageddon hypothesis. Once the appropriate meteorite or bomb had struck, surviving human beings would converge on Foulness Island, still no doubt moaning, as always, about the weather, the traffic, and the fireballs, all ready to start rebuilding human society in giant bunkers. Keeping the tube train running smoothly, an impossible enough task even in conditions of balmy peacetime, would help to keep them on their toes. Also, to the enthusiast's way of looking at things, as long as there were trains around, life would still be worth living.

Theory number two came from the wilder wings of FUM, from those members who had links with other activist groups like Nuclear Disarmament and Animal Liberation. Campaigns in the early 1980s against nuclear trains from Bradwell power station had produced a strange spattering of anarchist train-buffs, with some of the most unusual minds I have ever come across. They basically believed that the Foulness Underground was a giant plaything for the ruling classes. "You probably didn't know this," one radicalised FUM had told me, "but all those nuclear submarine commanders is train-buffs. They've all got big model railway sets on those submarines. The ordinary working-class sailors have to give up bunk space to make room for the track. That Underground is like a big club track for them to play with when they're on leave. Only they have to bury it underground so all you poor sorry tax-paying geezers don't kick up a rumpus. Once they've nuked the rest of us, they can all come ashore on Foulness and play trains happily for the rest of their lives. And since they're going to live for ever from all those injections of working class pituitary gland, that's going to be a long time." Radical FUMs also appeared to have a slightly different agenda from the others. Their vague aim was not so much to run the Underground, as to liberate one or two of the trains from their imprisonment by the ruling classes, and release them into the surrounding countryside.

I still wasn't sure that I believed in the Foulness tube-train, but then I never believed in fairies either, until I trod on one when I was walking in the woods and it told me in a beery voice to get lost.

If anything, Foulness was getting bleaker and more deserted as we approached Havengore Creek, the body of water that separates Foulness from the softy civilian mainland. My only companions were the occasional bits of hush-hush apparatus that had been set up alongside the sea-wall. Odd antennae winked and beeped, and on one occasion, I swear, tried to pinch Essex Dog's bottom. One item of gadgetry actually lay underwater, about three feet from the tide level. The headline "*Dead robot was love victim*" briefly flashed through my mind – but I'd sworn not to write about these things.

Essex Dog and I had walked four and a half miles by now, and although she was still enjoying the sunshine and exercise, I was becoming increasingly fidgety. All this time and distance, and yet nothing had gone wrong. There had been no adventures. And at this point, I started to look out to sea at the Broomway.

The Foulness Underground train might be a myth, but the Broomway is for real. The Broomway is one of the most extraordinary footpaths in Britain. I had a copy of the Foulness guide, by the Essex county archivist JR Smith in my pocket. I stopped to consult this again, although Smith's words were pretty well engraved in the part of my mind marked: "Walks Section – wipe your thoughts before entering."

"The Broomway," the archivist wrote, "is an ancient trackway which runs for a distance of six miles across the Maplin Sands, following the contour of the land about a quarter of a mile from the shore. The track derives its name from the hundreds of bunches of small poles or twigs buried in the sand and shaped like inverted besoms (witches brooms) which marked the seaward side of the track. ... When it was in regular use, the Broomway must surely have been the most dangerous road in England. ... About the time the seaward tide meets the Broomway, the shoreward one also touches it, and in the conflict as to which shall hold sway, swirling zones and miniature whirlpools are formed. In misty weather it is impossible to judge where the shore is from the direction of the tide and many unfortunate travellers have struggled out to sea to meet their deaths. ... In the parish registers of burials there are numerous mentions of parishioners and strangers found drowned."

The Broomway fell into disuse after World War I. Despite appeals put out in the newspaper, I'd not been able to find anybody alive who would admit to having walked or ridden along the Broomway, let alone flown one of those broomsticks above it. I had indeed toyed with the idea of walking it myself, as a fund-raising venture for my pet charity (the Royal Society for the Prevention of Yet More Charity Walks). Then my friend Terry Cotgrove, editor of the *Southend Observer*, stepped in. The Cotgroves have been sailors and fishermen since at least the seventeenth century, and Terry has sailed every inch of Estuary waters. "Don't try to walk the Broomway," he begged. "Just don't do it. You'll be doomed. If you must do something dangerous, get a reporting job in Kosovo, but don't try walking the Broomway. It's suicide."

I'd accepted what he said at the time, which was why we were now tamely walking the concrete sea-wall rather than paddling through the surf. But now, as we walked, I cast ever more wistful glances to sea. There was no longer any sign of the upright brooms that used to mark the Broomway. No doubt the last broom had long ago been filched for resale to sado-masochists. But several army amphibious DUKW vehicles had driven past at high speeds, by DUKW standards (about 4mph). The vehicles were clearly following the line of the old Broomway, so there must still be a solid surface, just under the water. OK, so it was a dangerous spot in a mist, but the weather was sunny and clear. Besides, even if I did get stuck in the mud, I had a mobile-phone, and what a story it would make. I would ring the newsdesk and the rescue services in that order, then settle comfortably into the mud, and in no time at all I would be appearing alongside Michael Buerk on Dial 999.

Alright, so it would be a bit naughty. But I had an excuse – the same one that I had seen countless yobs make to magistrates. I was fed up. I hadn't found anybody to interview all day and there just wasn't any other sort of trouble to be had in this unpopulated place.

I had just about made my mind up to walk out into the Estuary when all thoughts of the Broomway evaporated.

Suddenly, I saw it. *It!*

There, waving gently in the breeze, was the silver flower. The very one that the Foulness Underground Movement had talked about.

"Just look," they'd said, all those years ago, "for signs of the silver leaf. You'll see rows of them above the railway. There's no plant like them anywhere else. They grow where the ground's been disturbed when they dug the railway."

So the plants weren't some crackpot myth after all. They were for real. Moreover, the plants were just as they'd been described – like bits of Christmas tinsel on sticks. They were about two feet tall, grew in rows rather than clumps, and seemed to issue a strange, silvery internal light out of themselves as they caught the sea-breeze. I had never seen anything like them in a gardening career of almost inspired weed growing.

A sort of horticultural scavenging instinct kicked in. I wanted one of these plants as a keepsake. Also, if I pressed my ear to the ground next to the silver plant, I should be able to hear the rumblings of the 14.17 Foulness special. I might even be able to report what musical note pitch it rumbled in. I would be the trainspotting equivalent of the man who found the lost chord.

There was just one problem. The plants were all on the other side of the borrowdyke, the water-filled ditch between the sea-wall and the land. Still, it was a warm day and I didn't mind getting slightly wet in the interests of botany.

I was half way down the bank when I remembered the instructions. "Do not leave the path on any account. Foulness is a dangerous place." At this point I froze. I looked around. I realised with horror that the side of the earth bank where I had come to rest was a deadly killing ground. It glinted with half buried scraps of steel that were clearly land-mines and molehills that were clearly video observation posts. Right now, lots of security personnel, perched in front of monitors, were putting down the *Daily Star* and crying: "Thank God. At last we can finally get to shoot somebody!" As far as Foulness was concerned, I was an invading Speznatzi. The costume of a rundown pantomime journalist didn't fool anybody.

The top of the sea-wall was only about eight feet above my head, yet it might have been a mile away. Between me and safety lay gently purring landmines, and some coiled springs which I recognised as a job-lot arms purchase from Darth Vadar. Only then did the eye reach the top of the bank, where Essex Dog lay. Rather than follow me down the bank she had dozed off on the path. By now she had probably gone over to the enemy side.

I suddenly remembered why I had never become a war correspondent, apart from the fact that there aren't any wars to cover in Billericay or Southend, unless you count what happens at the bowls clubs. Basically, I was a born coward. And now, here I was, about to be vaporised by every secret anti-personnel weapon in the Western arsenal. Would anything be left of me? Some big bone, my pelvis perhaps, might survive the onslaught. I imagined the charred relic being presented to my wife by a couple of apologetic military policeman. I imagined her, incensed, laying about the MPs, perhaps using the pelvis to lam them on the helmets.

I was in the wrong, too. In the urge to find out more about that Underground railway, I'd broken the agreement and strayed off the Estuary path, into the grim hinterland of Foulness Island. Was there any way I could surrender? I needed something white to wave at whatever video cameras were watching. I thought about my underpants, but they were Jurassic Park ones with a snarling tyrannosaurus on them. This might send out the wrong message to the military.

And then, blind instinct took over. Forgetting landmines, forgetting everything except just getting back to the Thameside Path, I sprinted straight back up the bank and threw myself onto the top of the sea-wall, almost but not quite waking Essex Dog in the process.

I lay on the sea-wall in the sunshine, and gazed out over the Maplin Sands. I was alive! And still attached to my pelvis –

indeed, more emotionally attached than I'd ever realised.

At that point, the Estuary wilderness started to talk to me, for the first time since it had turned blue many years ago. Unwind, relax, stay calm man, it said. You'll learn what this walk is all about soon enough. You're off duty, son. Enjoy.

Old Man Thames was dead right, too. It was Saturday. I was on a walking holiday. I didn't need trains, subterranean or any other kind. Yet I was still trying to find, or if I couldn't find, make, news.

Ahead, about a mile away, the sea-wall curved inland, marking the landward tip of Foulness Island. It was a sort of learning curve, too. The Estuary path itself, this undiscovered highway, was all the story I needed. All I had to do was keep on walking, and I knew, somehow, I'd land the biggest story of my life. "Saddle up," I said to the dog. And so we set off for the Ness of Shoebury, and the official start and finish of the River Thames.

The actress Kate O'Mara, dressed for the kill as Queen Elizabeth I
for the 1988 Tilbury pageant

Four

Shoebury – The Name of the Nose

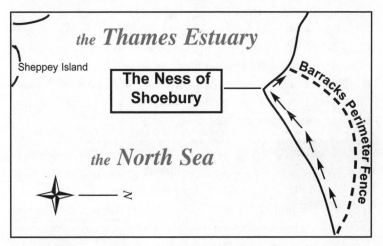

the **Thames Estuary**

Sheppey Island

The Ness of Shoebury

the **North Sea**

Barracks Perimeter Fence

N

ASKED to name the most spectacular stretch of scenery on the River Thames, most people who know the river, and a few who don't, would probably suggest Cliveden Reach. The Buckinghamshire beauty-spot is certainly a strong contender. The river curves round a high, beech-clad hill, topped by magnificent gardens and what is supposed to be the finest hotel in Britain. You sort of suspect, though, that the kind of researchers who compile this sort of statistic aren't paid enough to be allowed inside the hotel to check. Cliveden is also famous for the frolics of the Cliveden Set, whose antics scandalised Britain in the 1960s, and who were too busy, it is said, watching Christine Keeler floating at one end of the hilltop swimming pool, and her bikini top at the other, to be able to enjoy the scenery, poor things.

Call me Mr Biased, if you like, but there is a place on the Estuary that makes Cliveden look like a mound of EC surplus prunes. This is the Ness of Shoebury. It is the one point on the

Thames where you really understand the meaning of the word Estuary. Position yourself at one point on the Ness and you are standing on a river-bank. Step back one yard, and you are standing by the sea. (Note for those who slept through school geography lessons: the sea is the big one).

Ness means nose in a number of languages, mostly defunct like Old High Gothic, but including new low Southend. The Ness does indeed stick out into the Estuary like a snout. With the North Sea throwing itself against one side and the full surge of the Thames trying to push it out of the way on the other, it is, inevitably, a very wet one.

The reason that nobody lists the Ness in any Top of the Thameside Pops list is simple. For 150 years hardly a single civilian has set foot on the place. Like Foulness Island, the Ness of Shoebury has been sealed off by the military. The mile and a quarter of shoreline wrapped around the promontory is sealed off by a high brick wall, so that you can't even see the proboscis, let alone rub noses with it. For umpteen generations, one of the most illustrious landscapes in Britain has existed for the delectation of squaddies and their commanders alone.

Although they are both military establishments, Foulness and Shoebury are very different places. The Shoebury barracks exist as a world apart and they are certainly inaccessible. Journalists were seldom welcome. As a baby reporter I did consider enlisting, purely in order to write an expose (anything to get away from covering supermarket openings). Ultimately, I decided it would have spoilt the point of the exercise if I'd promptly been seconded to the Foreign Legion.

Yet, while reclusive, the Shoebury soldiery is hardly secretive. How could it be when it probably makes more noise than any other squad in the UK?

All through my childhood, twelve miles up-Estuary from Shoebury, the noise of things going boom and bang on the ranges was part of the familiar background to life. The whole landscape would shake as the big guns went off. People would comment on it in the same way they commented on the weather. "Heavy old day down Shoebury way," they'd mutter. A lot of things, from plagues of flies, to loose teeth, to wife-beating could be laid at the door of the Shoebury boom effect. Mrs Latimore, who ran a general store in Wickford, blamed the boom for knocking her husband's ashes off the shelf. "Mr L was a conscientious objector," she said. "I reckon they were getting even with him." Me, I always blamed it on the boom when my house-plants died of thirst.

What exactly was being blown up at Shoebury, nobody exactly knew. There was vague talk of testing big naval guns, although how they managed to winch all those aircraft-carriers over the walls of the base nobody ever could work out. It was also said that they destroyed lots of unwanted munitions that "had fallen into the wrong hands". You could always tell these explosions because they sounded foreign – thin wails and cringing thuds as against the manly earthquakes that represented the British explosions.

Life at Shoebury barracks was, by all accounts, exceedingly pleasant. Despite blowing up the equivalent of a nation-state or two every year, the camp had the reputation of a civilised, unstressed sort of place with a well-stocked library, a topping cricket team, and time to enjoy the Estuary views over an evening gin-and-tonic that started around 2.30pm. The commanding officer actually found time to talk to local nature clubs and women's institutes about topics like Feathered Friends of the Foreshore.

The barracks had another distinction. It was my favourite underworld contact, Nick "Sureshot" Rob, who first introduced me to the ballroom dancers. "Champion dancers is what they've got plenty of there," said Rob, fount of knowledge on all things down Shoebury way. "All the best dancers in the British forces find their way there. They always won all the forces' dancing prizes. They've got plenty of time to practise, see. And no danger of getting their toes run over by a tank. Those guys didn't shoot Nazis in the war, they tangoed with them until they begged to surrender."

The military prancers of Shoebury also – and to the eternal gratitude of our newspaper – generated a ghost. Any hint or suggestion of a ghost sighting used to be followed up avidly by my newspaper, especially in the August silly season, when stories of any sort, and particularly about the living, were hard to find. It never took much to get a ghost story together. A late night boozer making his way home is suddenly attacked by the ghost of a privet hedge. A night watchman hears a low moaning from the factory post-room. Out of such simple incidents are headlines made that read: *"Ghost blamed for haunting horror."* Often this would be accompanied by a blurred double-exposure shot of a journalist in a sheet, purporting to be the ghost, posing momentarily for his local rag in mid-stalk.

The Shoebury ghost took the guise of a Victorian subaltern in a forage cap. A small, domed pavilion juts out from the barracks, overlooking the foreshore. It was here that the ghost – or puff of colliding kittiwakes or whatever it was that caused the illusion – was glimpsed. Lieutenant Willy the Wallflower, as he was swiftly dubbed, was leaning over the pavilion rail, moodily puffing a cheroot. In no time, a story had accrued round him. Leg blown off in the Afghan campaigns – had to sit the dances out at the Colonel's ball – girl he loved stolen away by foxtrotting colleague – gets trusty batman to beat him to death with his own wooden leg. The story would never have made the editions in the sober months, but in August anything goes, and in it went.

Willy the ghost was just about believable, but who could swallow the story of the ballroom? Rob told me about this as well. "The finest ballroom in Britain is there in the Horseshoe Barracks, my friend," he told me. "It's got gold leaf on the walls and it's just plastered with Old Master paintings. Shove one of those down your tutu and flog it to this connoisseur geezer in Canning Town and you're set up for life. I'd be in there, I tell you, if half the bloody British army wasn't in the way. How they got to build somewhere like that I don't know, but I reckon there's a few drapes and things in that ballroom that are down in the books as Howitzers."

Rob tended to be about fifty per cent reliable, and I reckoned this information was part of the bent half. You didn't have to look very long and hard at the outside of the Shoebury barracks, with its grim walls, and grimmer barracks buildings just inside, and even grimmer sergeants at the gate, and even grimmer sergeant's mums bringing their offspring their lunch in pails, to realise this place meant business. This was Shoebury, where they handled the biggest explosions this side of a wonky Texan barbecue. This was the town of the booms that could shatter a set of nancy boy's nerves twenty miles away. If a Jane Austen ballroom did happen to find its way here, the gunners would use it for target practice.

Then, around 1997, something happened, or rather, stopped happening, in Shoebury. The big booms ceased. For one and a half centuries, the Shoebury boom had been shaking the Estuary landscape, and suddenly it wasn't there any more. It wasn't long before there was talk about putting a preservation order on it. Conservationists wondered whether they could get the National Trust to take an interest in shaking up their scenery with the odd historic explosion, or perhaps even a Festival of Ye Olde Shell Fire.

The reason for the doom of the boom was soon apparent. The Ministry of Defence was shutting down the Horseshoe Barracks, and selling the land. I had mixed feelings. It was sad to see the end of yet another military tradition. On the other hand, it did mean that I might finally get to walk the length of shoreline around the Ness of Shoebury. And I might just be the first civilian to do so since Queen Victoria had curves. It would also, of course, mean that I could incorporate it into the Thames Estuary Trail I was just starting to stitch together

I rang the Ministry of Defence at Goojerat Barracks in Colchester and in due course Warrant Officer Mike Smith contacted me. Mike was the Royal Engineer now responsible for maintenance of the old barracks site, and, yes, he would be happy to conduct me and Essex Dog along the one and a half miles of shoreline occupied by the barracks site. So, at last, on another fine day, I made my way through the picket-gate at the end of Shoebury High Street – and stepped straight into an extraordinary lost world.

On one side of the gate was ordinary, shabby Shoebury. On the other, Xanadu – an undiscovered chunk of garden city. Terraces of elegant town houses ran alongside broad streets. In between were what had, until recently, clearly been immaculate lawns and strips of turf – as immaculate as only squaddies on punishment duty can keep a bit of turf. A crescent of magnificent officers' houses centred on a soaring clock-tower. Tall specimen trees lined the streets. The place amounted to a perfect early Victorian town, with nothing to indicate that the twentieth century had ever had permission to start marching, let alone that it was about to croak its last. For 150 years, life had gone its own way in these barracks, safely mummified and inured from the outside world by high walls on three sides, by the sea on the fourth, and with possibly the world's largest concentration of artillery power primed to keep the realities of ordinary life such as Jehovahs' Witnesses at bay.

We had arrived at just the right time in history – time to catch Sleeping Beauty's barracks at their most evocative. The last few regular occupants (a Catering Corps unit) had just departed. The builders had not yet moved in. The cricket pitch and the superb flower-borders (not a pansy in site, we noted) were overgrown but not yet infiltrated by undergrowth. The mid-Victorian buildings were intact and unaltered. Something unbelievable had happened. In my own suburban patch, I had stumbled on a vast, unguessed-at ghost town. Through the passageways between the barrack blocks, I glimpsed the Estuary. "See, I told you I had a few surprises in store," it said, in that irritating manner it had started to acquire.

Mike Smith was a archetypical military man, open and friendly, but carrying the unmistakeable message: "Don't even think you can blarney, waffle or cow-piddle me, my friend." He was also, fortunately really under the circumstances, a keen walker, although his style of pedestrianism was quite different from my own. The dog and I favoured a relaxed amble, me poking my nose into as many places as possible where it wasn't wanted along the way, and the dog pretending to look embarrassed. Mike favoured gruelling forty-mile non-stop hauls. A good walk by his standards was defined as one that he survived to walk away from.

It was fortunate that Mike actually liked walking, because much of his work consisted of the stuff. Mike was the lone human being responsible for the Horseshoe Barracks, officer in-command of the ghost town. At fortnightly intervals he would march (and marches still) along the one and a half miles of the barracks sea-wall. On this occasion, Essex Dog and I joined him.

The North Sea was throwing itself with some force against the wall as we set out. After a few yards, Mike stopped, and pointed at a spot on the wall. During the fortnight since Mike's last visit, the waves had taken another slab of concrete as a souvenir of Southend.

"There's usually some new item of damage like that each time I come here," he said.

"Do you mend it yourself?" I asked, hopefully. Already the "intro" paragraph for a story was forming in my mind.

"*All that stands between Essex and a deluge of tidal destruction,*" it read, "*is one brave, underpaid soldier, a lonely figure, working with his bare hands to stem the force of the oceans.*"

But no, I suppressed it. I had sworn to give headlines and news stories a miss on this walk.

Anyway, Mike's reply was deeply disappointing. "No, stupid," he said (or that's how I remember it). "A gang comes and sorts it out."

We walked on a little further. I tried some polite small talk. "Do you have far to come, Mike?" I asked.

"Leicestershire," he said. "Leicestershire – Colchester – Shoebury."

"But that must be about 150 miles!"

"Almost," said Mike tersely. "But that's how it is in the army today."

With irresistible force, another intro paragraph sprang up in my mind.

"Feeling safe, Shoeburyites? Confident the 1953 floods could never repeat themselves? Sure you're not going to wake up in the morning and find your bed bobbing in an Amsterdam canal. And your wife being offered something suspect by a Dutch druggie? Well think again. 'Cos the man in charge of sea-wall watching is tucked up in his own bed in Leicestershire. That's right. Leicestershire in the Midlands. It's 140 miles away and it doesn't even have a coastline."

I was interrupted at this point by the lone Leicester soldier himself. "There seems to be something the matter with your dog," he said.

Essex Dog, who had been bounding ahead, had suddenly stopped in her tracks as if she'd encountered a snake with the shape of the King Charles spaniel from next door half way down its tummy. Her hackles had risen, her bony tail had disappeared into the folds of her well-rounded girth.

She was standing next to a structure that looked vaguely familiar. It took a second or two to identify it. Then I realised that it was the gazebo, haunting ground of Lieut Willy the Wallflower. The little building is set into the seawall, jutting out over the beach, though the only access is from the barracks path, in the forbidden zone. The photograph that had appeared in the paper had been taken from the foreshore, about 300 yards away – as close as the photographer was allowed to get. This was the first time I had seen it close up. Willy the ghost was nowhere to be seen. Perhaps it was his lunch hour. Or per-

haps he just knew that there's no such thing as ghosts. Yet
something was frightening the dog.

If Mike had possessed a proper sense of occasion, the next
thing he should have said was: "My God, I've been in some
sticky situations, I've had my throat cut by Indonesian pirates
and my balls lassoed by the terrible women warriors of Sumatra,
but I've never know sheer terror until this moment." Or at the
very least he could have given me the quote: "Your dog looks
as if she's seen a ghost."

In fact, he just said: "Better see what she wants, hadn't you?"

I crouched down beside the dog, who by now was trembling.
"She looks as if she's seen a ghost," I said. Somebody had to say it.

Mike politely stifled a snort of disdain.

"You can imagine it, though, can't you," I said, determined
to get some sort of news story out of this matter-of-fact military
engineer. "The ghost of some poor subaltern, smoking a last
cigar on the gazebo. Ever seen anything like that, Mike, when
you've been patrolling the sea walk at the end of the world? You
must have seen something you can't explain, eh, eh?"

"No, can't say I have," said Mike. But then he said something that knocked me back far more than any ghost story.
"Would you like to see the ballroom?" he asked.

"Ballroom?" I gasped. "I thought that was some sort of myth.
I don't believe in ballrooms."

"Ballroom, officers' mess, call it what you like," he said. "It's
worth seeing."

Leaving Essex Dog tethered as far from the gazebo as possible, I followed Mike through a rather inconspicuous door in the
main building, along a corridor and, from there into what must
surely be the most amazing room on the Estuary.

The furniture had all been removed and there were faint
patches on the walls where huge oil-portraits of colonels had
once hung, and even bigger paintings of Johnny Foreigner having his teeth blasted out by Shoebury patent artillery. If anything, this just served to highlight the enormous dimensions of

the ballroom, and the great sweep of the dance floor. The place smelt like no other room I had ever been inside. It was a mingled whiff of beeswax, very old brandy and, if I hadn't known better, old cigar smoke. Yet while there were ghost smells, there was no ghost music. The huge room was still and silent. But outside, you could hear the noise of the Estuary, breaking against the sea-wall. "You think you're Mr Smart, don't you," it said. "You think you've seen it all. I tell you, you ain't seen nothin' yet."

I made a mental note to apologise to Sureshot Rob for my cynicism.

We emerged into the sunshine to continue the walk, and I bent down to release Essex Dog. A soon as I had unclipped her, she shot off like a bolt out of a crossbow. Her destination was about fifty yards off, a low building, sunk into the cricket-pitch. She reached it and began scrabbling and scratching at the door. I called to her a couple of times, and rustled a crisp packet, normally a sure summons. This time, it failed. So I ate the crisps anyway and went to fetch her.

"What is that place, Mike?" I asked.

"It's the old air-raid shelter. People in the main block could get to it in a few seconds if there was an attack."

As we walked, I pondered why Essex Dog should have wanted to get into that shelter. Was the attraction based on something inside the shelter, like a 1940 spam sandwich? Or was she trying to escape from something. Being logically minded, she would naturally have chosen the shelter as the safest spot. She certainly looked like a dog who was about to be dive-bombed by some hot-shot cat·fancier.

At least the dog cheered up, as we put more distance between ourselves and the gazebo and ballroom. We passed the magnificent commandant's house, the shell storage dump – now an overgrown waste, swarming with rabbits – and a huge concrete gun emplacement. Then we reached a rather dilapidated jetty, at which point the path veered to the right. We had reached the Ness of Shoebury.

Mike was all for carrying on without so much as slacking our pace. But I asked if we could stop for a few seconds. I wanted mentally to compose the opening paragraph for the fancy two-page article I was writing about this experience, to be grandly titled: Walking into Secret Shoebury.

"*I stood there, awestruck,*" my brain dictated to another bit of itself which could handle shorthand. "*Possibly the first civilian in a century and a half to stand at the point where Old Father Thames begins and ends his life. For years I had dreamed of this place, yet nothing quite prepares you for the impact of the scene. On one side you have a river, contained, tied into the land. Incline your head a mere twenty degrees and suddenly the most famous waterway of old England has ceased to be, has swollen into the dimensions of an ocean. The view as the land sweeps away on either side, to make ready for the parting of the ways, is so glorious on a fine day that you want to invite the whole world here to gawp.*"

Great stuff, I thought to myself. That should earn brownie points and an extra cup of tea at the local writers' circle. Yet something didn't quite ring true. The view was astonishing, no doubt about that. But there was no way that the Ness itself, with its neglected jetty and its ratty brick hut was going to set anybody's soul on fire, except perhaps a Rentokil executive's.

It was typical, of course, of the Estuary, that its most important site should be studiously neglected. It went with everything else about this run-down, underfunded, fenced-off, shabby, low-key latitude, a place inhabited by plain folk who got on with things and didn't go in for showy gestures – a bit like my companion, in fact.

There wasn't much time to think all this through, however. Not only was Mike keen to be on the march again, but Essex Dog had started to howl and grizzle. She, clearly, was not a fan of the Ness.

We strode on for another few hundred yards, until at last we came to the perimeter fence. On the other side stood the old

coastguard station, and beyond that, free passage, where anybody could walk alongside the Estuary. Soon, though, the
perimeter fence will be torn down. The world and his wife and
their marriage guidance councillor will be able to walk the old
barracks site. But by then hundreds of houses will cover the site
and it will no longer be a ghost city, and even psychic dogs will
cease to whimper.

We had to turn back at this stage, though not before I had
noted down twenty points for the best-constructed frustration
I'd met yet. If you truly want to foul a footpath, get a Victorian
military engineer to do it for you. (I fondly imagined that this
was the last such frustration I would encounter on the Estuary.
How wrong can you be?)

We retraced our steps. I said goodbye to Mike at the barracks gate, then strolled down Rampart Street, following the
line of the high barracks wall to the foreshore. At this point the
wall extends across the beach in the form of a breakwater, festooned with dire warnings not to venture onto the foreshore in
front of the barracks. This was, no doubt, a most sensible pre-
caution. Even if strollers didn't get blown up, the gunners' language when they missed their target could ruin any granny's
holiday.

A few families were gambolling on the beach, but none of
them had crossed the forbidden breakwater into the military
zone. The message clearly hadn't got out that the barracks were
closed and empty, or that the foreshore, at the end of the day,
remained a right of way.

It certainly hadn't reached the little knot of treasure-
hunters who were gathered in a knot near the water's edge.
They had two metal-detectors and a mound of lager-cans
between them. Their attempts at metal-detecting seemed pretty half-hearted. At one stage they even gave up trawling the
beach, and amused themselves by running the metal-detectors
over the beer-cans, presumably to see if different brands of lager
created different squeaks from the machine.

They couldn't have been having much luck. The beach must have been trawled many times over, right down to the last mollusc attempting to mate with the last discarded ring-pull. Yet on the far side of the breakwater lay what must be uncharted territory for treasure-hunters. No doubt the treasure-seekers were kept out by fear of the shock of actually finding something worthwhile, or that any treasure might blow them and their instruments to kingdom come. Much safer to stick to lager cans. Lager doesn't blow up metal detectors, not even the stuff they make in Glasgow.

I could never afford a metal-detector, though I had a vague, unspecified dream that I might one day find a nice one buried somewhere. Yet a few weeks later, Essex Dog and I were back on Shoebury beach, this time in the forbidden military zone, conducting our own search for metal objects with our bare hands.

In the interim, I had conducted an interview with a remarkable World War II military expert from Canvey Island, John D'Agastino. John had arrived for our meeting with a case-load of junk. There were hundreds of lumps of rusted, twisted metal all culled from the Estuary mud-flats. I had scrutinised these all with an informed eye, but there was nothing there that seemed of remote use to any decent scavenger – not even to file for the family's ration of dietary iron shavings (some of my womenfolk veer towards anaemia).

In John's magician's hands, however, these useless, unrecognisable little bits of metal slowly transformed into something quite remarkable – the flight-deck panel of a World War II Flying Fortress.

"There were two of them that crashed out there in the Estuary," John explained. "There's lots of bits lying out there in the mud if you know what you're looking for." He held up what was quite obviously the sub-membrane to the altimeter of a Series Three. Only an oaf would refer to it as a rusty, postage-stamp-sized piece of sheet metal encrusted with mud and fossilised crab-phlegm.

If my interviewee had had just a few more of those bits of twisted metal, he would have been able to fly home. He had created marvels like this out of the Canvey mudflats, an area that can hardly be described as unfilleted by treasure-seekers. Indeed, it can resemble a beachcombers' convention on days when the mud is squelchy and yielding up its secrets. If Canvey could do this, what excitements must the virgin, unexplored beach at Shoebury offer! There should be enough there to supplement a poverty-stricken journalist's income for years. The very worst-case scenario was that we would dig up cheaper pickings on items like army-surplus slippers than we could ever obtain from a jumble-sale.

Our optimism proved fully justified. Within half an hour, we had a already acquired a number of treasures. There was a rusty bayonet, quite an up-to-date bicycle pedal, an enamelled hamster bath, a trowel (this actually helped us to work a bit faster) and a small anchor – or it might have been a grappling-hook for some blithe cavalier trying to break into the Wrens' quarters.

It was then that I encountered The Object.

I knew right away that the Estuary had thrown up something special this time, because as soon as she spotted and sniffed it, Essex Dog began to bay. It was the same heart-breaking whingeful noise that she had used when passing the Ness.

The baying transformed into a fierce bark as I approached the mystery object. She was clearly telling me to stay away. All the better reason to examine it.

The thing consisted of a twisted metal-frame, sticking out of the mud. Clearly, most of the object was still buried. It was made up of rusty, heavily encrusted wrought-iron bars, topped by what looked like the remains of several fleur-de-lys. Something about it said: I am an item of military hardware and I take myself very seriously – you can call me Sir.

I have lost count of the number of times we have published warnings in the paper about the dangers of unexploded munitions. If you spot something that could be an old bomb or shell, or even bullet, leave it alone, call the police, we urged. On no account touch it, let alone take it home to show to the new baby.

Yet now that I found myself in just such a position, the temptation to turn my back on all that good advice was irresistible. I wanted to hammer the object or dance up and down on it. At the very least, I thought, I could chuck a brick at it from a safe distance. If there was an explosion and I survived, I could then dash off a self-righteous column in the newspaper about how negligent it was for the Council to leave things like this lying around. It might also be the chance to create the last ever Shoebury big boom to rattle half of Essex.

It looked as if, once again, the Estuary had produced the goods. Or was there a more sinister scenario? There had been such a profound sense of destiny in all my recent dealings with the Estuary. Was it out to get me? Would the last Shoebury boom be me?

At last, very delicately, I began to pick at the mud and sand round the mystery object. Some twenty minutes later I was three or four inches lower, and the object was looking even more mysterious. There was a lacework of parallel bars. Some were missing, some bent, some rusted, and some in fine fettle. They formed a vague bell shape. But there was nothing inside.

With increasing excitement, I put out a call on my mobile phone (no, I hadn't scavenged that from the beach; it's one of the few objects I've actually bought). I wanted to pick the brains of another expert beachcomber, name of Smith (yes, really). This was a guy who actually made a living by selling the stuff he scavenged. Some of his discoveries have gone to the British Museum. If anybody could identify the mystery object, it had to be him.

Smith answered the phone after eight or ten rings. "Yes, what is it?" he asked testily. In the background, I could hear some excited female giggling.

"I've dug up this incredible thing and I know it will make a great story," I said.

The giggling at the other end of the phone was turning into a deep, luxuriant sighing.

"You ring me up at a time like this to describe some old rubbish," he snarled.

"It's not rubbish. It's really interesting." I tried to describe it to him, against an increasing background noise of sighing and grunting. "You couldn't make your way down here now, could you?"

"It's probably a parrot cage," he said, and put the phone down.

Somewhat indignant at the treatment I had received, I carried on digging. Alas, the object increasingly petered out into an anticlimax. It might just have been the top part of a parrot's cage, but any base had rotted away many long years ago. The bars just tapered into rusty points. This thing wouldn't have held an ostrich, let alone a parrot.

After that, I rather lost heart, and went home for dinner. Still, I had at least made a discovery about Essex Dog. The simple fact was that she hated History. She was a party animal, she liked loud disco music, and flash gadgets. But she could not take anything ancient. That was why she had been so unhappy outside the historic ballroom, and why she so despised the object I had tried to dig up. Her disquiet at the Ness was harder to explain, but maybe her hatred of history also extended to scenery. If so, she would be a useful device on the path ahead of us. She could be used to gauge the quality of the scenery and the authenticity of anything that claimed to be historic. If it upset Essex Dog, then it was A1 quality.

The notion of history set me to thinking about those endangered species, flotsam, jetsam and driftwood. The ships on the Estuary these days tend to be either container vessels or floating bingo parlours. People aboard ship don't drop things overboard any more, apart from the occasional set of false teeth when they're gawping at a view. What will there be on the shorefront to entice our grandchildren when they in their turn become beachcombers? It is all very well to take what we can from the beach, but shouldn't we also be thinking in terms of leaving something behind in our turn?

As luck would have it, I was soon afterwards able to do something about this. I was also able, simultaneously, to erect a monument on the Ness of Shoebury, thus killing two birds with one stone.

In a junkshop in Leigh, I came across an old, unused plaque. It consisted of a brass plate on a polished, ogee-shaped mounting. I purchased this for a small consideration. I then had the plate engraved with the following words: *The Ness Monument, until a better one comes along. Here begins and ends the River Thames.*

Early one morning I tiptoed along the beach and placed this on the Ness, just above tide level.

Then I waited for somebody to discover it and send in a photograph to my newspaper. We could then run a story under the headline: *Miniature Ness monument loched in mystery.*

Nobody, though, has contacted us yet. Maybe the Estuary waters have washed the plaque away. Maybe, some other puzzled beachcomber has taken it home.

Maybe, though, it sits there still – until some better monument does, indeed, come along.

The shattered remnants of a concrete path are the nearest thing to a monument at Warden Point, the crumbling outpost of civilisation that marks the beginning and end of the Thames Estuary on the Kent side

Dickens country pub – the Rose & Crown at Allhallows

Five

Southend – the Teeming Mud

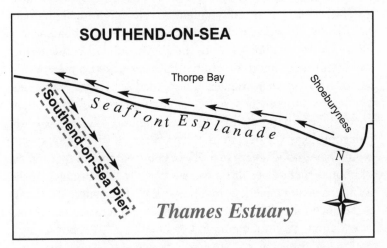

JUST A FEW inches made all the distance. On the far side of the barracks' perimeter fence, the Estuary walk entered a different world. The sense of ancient secrecy vanished, and in its place surged all the delights of the English seaside, with its crowds, food, noise and Pokemon airbeds. Essex Dog's tail rose high as she caught her first whiff of sun-tan oil. She knew the score. Ten o'clock on a fine weekday morning. Scores of mums and a spattering of house-husbands would have safely packed their charges off to school, and now be asleep in the sun. She would have the sun-tan oil licked off their legs before they had the chance to wake and scream, let alone organise a petition against the Council's decision to disband the mobile dog service.

The four miles of seafront between the Southend districts of West Shoebury and Chalkwell represent the only real attempt at creating a holiday resort on the Estuary, unless you count the disused mudbaths at Allhallows, which always had a disconcerting habit of swallowing health-seekers whole. Human beings in bathing costumes have a worse deal in terms of habitat than the rare bar-tailed godwit or the Pomeranian skua.

Thousands of years ago, it was a different story. Around 4,000BC these low, dull flatlands were a veritable human metropolis for people in fur swimming trunks, or, in days when clothes were for wimps, less. In the 1930s, builders constructing the brand new suburb of Thorpe Bay, unearthed some curious discoveries – numerous piles of discarded sea-shells. Such piles would not normally be a source of great interest, even to other oysters, but these shells told a compelling tale, at least to palaeontologists. Back in the days when such bone-experts would have stood a very real risk of being eaten and spat out as old bones themselves, little gaggles of early homo-sapiens performed a remarkable feat in Thorpe Bay. They survived. They lacked even the skill to make stone axes and scrapers (we think of early man as resourceful and practical, but the bodgers also had to live somewhere). Yet they contrived to exist on the foreshore, that thin margin between the terror of the sea and the horror of the forest. While these bodgers might have lacked the practical skills to construct Stonehenge, even in flatpack form, they survived at least long enough to build up some impressive mounds of shells. Neither fish nor forest themselves, they must have huddled in the sea winds and even envied the whelks and mussels their housing arrangements.

Oddly enough, no human bones were discovered in Thorpe Bay. The shore-dwellers must have moved on or been swept out to sea, or been vaporised by a particularly violent bout of seafood poisoning. The remains of their diet proved more enduring than they did. But at least they could lay claim to be the original Essex Men. Their direct descendants were the first people I met on the seafront.

Nothing much happened then for the next 4,000 years until Thorpe Bay was developed as an upmarket suburb, as usual, totally ignoring the sea. One third of the place is a golf-course, a very successful one. Its managers have regularly gone on to run the Royal and Ancient. But the club has fought shy about publicising this fact, in case residents become too excited.

For all its wealth of expensive houses, Thorpe Bay is a surprisingly bleak place, haunted by the sense of being on the road to nowhere. Even rowdy seafront cruisers don't usually make it this far. "It's meant for the quiet life. Nothing ever happens there," a local estate-agent told me in a rare, unguarded moment, adding: "I reckon all that boringness adds about £10,000 to the value of properties."

In fact, Thorpe Bay isn't as boring as all that. The houses may do their best to look regimented, but behind their facades the human goings-on are anything but uniformly grey. I cast my mind back to some of the stories I had covered in Thorpe Bay down the years.

I remembered the martinet who ran an amateur drama society for over twenty years. "Actually I never really cared much for the theatre and that sort of thing," he said, "and I never allowed myself to be seen on stage. But somebody had to maintain a bit of discipline with all those acting types or there's no knowing what would have happened."

Then there was the Ferrari dealer and vehicle collector who specialised in the extremes of transport. He drove the fastest production-car in town, albeit pretty carefully, since running into the back of a milk-float would instantly have shaved tens of thousands off the car's value, and millions off its street-cred.

By way of contrast, he then acquired the slowest vehicle in Southend, a school-bus that took almost four minutes to accelerate from nought to thirty. "It's a funny thing, but when I'm looking for a good time I actually think I spend more time driving that bus than my Ferraris," he told me. As an extra flourish, he then added to his collection a new superlative – the longest car in Britain. This was a stretch limousine, former property of the American embassy, specially acquired for a visit by President Bill Clinton. It was long enough to lay an entire chorus line of cabaret dancers end to end, although there was absolutely no proof that the amorous president had time on his brief visit to Britain to use it for this purpose. This limo had once, single-handedly, frozen traffic throughout central London when it attempted to turn into a narrow alleyway in Soho.

I left the seafront briefly to walk up Thorpe Hall Avenue. I passed under the railway bridge and stopped outside a house in Acacia Drive. Here had lived and died an ancient, corpulent City businessman. Now some celestial cumulus cloud buckles under the weight of all those Corporation lunches and dinners. "I always found the walk to the station something of a strain," he'd told me. "But I thought, what's the use of having a back garden that backs onto the railway-line if you can't make good use of the facility. So I came to a little arrangement with the train-drivers and they always stopped there for me. My wife carried a step-ladder so that I could get up to the carriage and nobody ever seemed to mind."

The best thing of all about Thorpe Bay is that its very title is a misnomer. There is no bay at Thorpe Bay, unless you count the artificial enclosure formed by Southend pier to the west and Shoebury Ness to the east. That is exactly what the developers chose to do, since bays sell better than straight lines. For that matter, the telephone directory lists no Thorpes as living in Thorpe Bay, either. The slightly uneasy subterfuge of its name somehow suits this place. No, Thorpe Bay is not dull.

The seafront for the first two miles is lined with beach-huts. Built in the 1920s and 30s, these little dwellings started life modestly enough as shelters against the searing Estuary wind, a rude breeze which has always displayed a vile habit of whipping the modesty-towels out of fat ladies' fingers as they scrambled into their swimming costumes. The arrival of the beach-huts saved many a granny's blushes, but nobody was going to confuse these rows of identikit sheds with a Riviera villa. Until the 1960s, it was commoner to see a clutch of bicycles parked outside a beach-hut than a car. When it rained, many of the bicycles got pride of place on the inside, while the families drank tea in the wet until it was time to cycle home.

Times have changed for the beach-hut. Their price on the market is rising at a faster rate than the mansions of Thorpe Bay. Two years ago, I'd heard somebody announce that he had purchased one as "a promising bricks and mortar investment." However shrewd a financial move, it seemed an odd way of looking at a hut made of wood. My Estuary walk on this particular morning was to be combined with a fact-finding mission about the new-found kudos of the Southend beach-hut, to be headed: *From shack to status symbol: Humble huts head into orbit.*

I struck paydirt immediately, in the shape of an actuary from Billericay who had bought a beach-hut because she was fed up with waiting around at Gatwick for flights to her Caribbean villa. "Anyway, everybody's got tropical pads these days. We thought about Whitstable, but that's been just a bit too discovered, don't you think?"

"And," she added, as a sort of moral self-justification, "it's an investment, isn't it?"

Armed with quotations and figures from this source, I put away my notebook. The rest of the day could be devoted to some serious walking.

Three miles ahead to the west we could see the celebrated, wondrous, decaying mass of Southend pier, the focal point of the Estuary, the world's longest pier, and the council's biggest headache. It's known in some quarters as the Mayor's Nightmayor, since nobody wants to go down in history as the person in charge on the day the pier finally upends and gives up the ghost – especially if they happen to be leading an official delegation along it at the time.

It should have been a swift and easy progress to the pier, but the human distractions were overpowering. The traditional English seaside is supposed to be a lost cause. Maybe so, but the crowds busy disporting themselves on the Estuary clearly hadn't found the time to read the obituaries gazetted in *Dead Duck*

Clarion. Everywhere I looked there was a tale to be told.

An athletic-looking dad and his son were arguing fiercely over the score in a game of beach-cricket. "You just can't stand to lose, can you dad," snorted the 10-year-old.

Two gay men had unfolded an elaborate picnic, and were now playfully pinging Marks & Spencer cherry tomatoes at one another.

A huge, very ill-looking man lay asleep on a sun-lounger, covered with blankets. We had read reports about the increasing frequency of dead whales washed up on these shores. Was this one of them, covered up with blankets and then forgotten by the council works department? No, it was definitely human, but for a brief moment we wondered whether he was dead. Essex Dog was all for licking him, but the shock of such an experience, while conceivably reviving, might just have quelled any last lingering spark of life. Fortunately, at this point the "corpse" broke wind, lingeringly and mournfully, then grunted with satisfaction. He lived! A conscientious reporter would have woken him up and asked if he had any horror stories concerning the local health authority. But we had an entire Estuary to cover. We hurried on.

We had to stop, however, when we encountered the old couple with the barbecue.

She must have been eighty if she was a day, older than even the most venerable hamburger for sale with onions on the seafront. She was labouring over the alfresco equivalent of a hot stove, a freestanding metal barbecue – quite a swanky one, too, with a designer label on it. Smoke was pouring from the charcoal. In the thick of it, coughed and spluttered the old lady. You'd have thought that the barbecue was providing enough destructive smoke to satisfy a pop festival, but she was laying on extra fumes from the end of a cigarette that jutted from the corner of her mouth.

"King. *Echo*. I'm thinking of doing an article about seaside barbecues," I said, hastily improvising.

"Well don't come to me, dear," she wheezed. "I'm no blessed good at it, as you can see. Nor's he, lazy old devil, he is." She indicated her husband, who was sitting on a deckchair, reading the *Sun*.

"Howdo," he said, nodding. "Don't let her give you one of her sausages, whatever you do. They've ruined many a good man." He cackled, then went back to reading his paper. "Don't listen to him. Go on, have a sausage, darling." I declined. It's always a bad sign when Essex dog doesn't try to raid a barbecue.

"Having a lunchtime barbecue?" I enquired.

"It's for the youngsters," said the old lady. "Can't see the point of the wretched things meself. Makes me feel like old Mother Cavewoman. It's me son asked me to do it. He's coming with the wife and kids after work, and he's told us to get the barbecue ready for the evening, and then we're all going to have a party."

"It's a bit early in the day to get started, isn't it?"

"You know the old cook's saying. Start with the dew, perfect stew," she announced.

I peered through the smoke at the meat on the barbecue, which did indeed vaguely resemble army surplus stew, right down to the cunning mottled green camouflage. "It's not quite the same with a barbecue as with a stew," I said, cautiously.

"This isn't your usual barbecue rubbish. I'm not cooking any of that hamburger nonsense they stuff down their throats these days," she said. "Only reason I agreed to do this is to get some decent food down my grandchildren's tums. I bet you don't even know what that is."

I peered at the wicked looking meat on the barbecue grid. It leered back contemptuously and tried to spit a goblet of fat up my nose.

"That," said the old lady, "is Scrag End. Me and the old man over there owe our fine state of fettle to that stuff. We couldn't afford steak or posh sausages when we was young. But if you knew your cuts of meat, you could live like a ruddy king."

A vivid picture was forming in my mind, as I imagined the children confronting the scorched scrag. "Will they eat it?" I asked. "My kids won't even touch toast unless it's got a sell-by date stamped in it."

"That's no worry, dear," she promised. "The secret is to make it sound appetising."

"How do you do that?"

"I just tell them that I've got a nice slice of Granny's scrag."

There wasn't much that I could say to this, and anyway, I felt that the cuts of meat that she favoured would probably be banned from mention on the recipe page of a family newspaper. So Essex Dog and I wandered down to the water's edge to watch the bathers. There were a surprising number of them making merry in the waves – surprising considering that the Estuary seawater was its usual colour and texture – a sort of watery equivalent of scrag-end. Indeed, I was sure that I could identify one patch as my own property. It had emerged from the family dishwasher only a couple of days ago and twelve miles upriver. Some of the bathers were children, but there was also a spattering of middle-aged men and women. I wondered whether these were hotshot lawyers. Sensible bathers do not take a dip off the Estuary beaches these days unless they take a solicitor into the water with them.

Southend came into being as a giant outdoor bathroom. For most of history it consisted of nothing more than a few oyster-men's cottages straddled along the seafront and a lonely tavern, the Britannia Inn (the Britannia still exists, although it is next to one of Southend's busiest roundabouts and loneliness is the least of its problems). Then, Princess Charlotte, only child of King William IV, and heir to the throne, came to stay here in 1801, hence the "Royal" bit. To exploit her visit, an elegant block of apartments, the Royal Terrace, just as remote and iso-lated as the Britannia but with better plumbing, was construct-ed on the cliff-tops. Londoners could make their way here by mail-coach or river to avail themselves of the wholesome sea-breezes, those blistering winds that continue to shrivel outdoor pot-plants all over the Estuary. The Royal Terrace is still with us, but Princess Charlotte is not. Alarmingly for Southend's reputation, she died not long after taking the waters. Not for the last time, the Estuary was suspected of murder. Although childbirth was the official reason given for her demise, suspicion lingered about the effect of Southend saline, and has never quite gone away. Perhaps somebody should have explained to Caroline that invalids should swim in the sea rather than drink it. In any case, the royal connection was quietly dropped, while Southend found its niche in life as the country's most blissfully downmarket resort.

The London, Tilbury and Southend railway provided the old East End with its quickest and cheapest route to the sea. A special offer ticket cost less than a trip to the public baths. Tens of thousands of EastEnders took advantage of this, and there was also a special "Swimmers' Express" at 6pm, allowing City businessmen to shoot down to the coast for a quick dip, and the chance to catch shrimps in their bowler-hats if they felt peckish. About 100 yards offshore floated Absalon's Marine Bathing Establishment, a giant covered barge. By all accounts it was a villainous, festering craft that threatened to flounder at any time. But it offered the cheapest changing facilities on the coast, along with a covered pool for those who objected to being rained on when they were swimming. As a very old lady, Mr Absalon's niece Connie described the place to me, as it was in its Edwardian heyday. "You'd see grown men cry with relief when they jumped in that water and felt the dirt of the London streets coming off them," she recalled.

Times and trains and drains all changed, and the Estuary lost its job as a bathroom. This was partly because Londoners had acquired showers, but also because of the fact that, by the 1960s, if you took a dip in the Estuary you came out of the water dirtier than when you went in. The term Oil Crisis had a different significance along the Estuary to other places.

Elsewhere it meant a shortage of oil. In Southend, it meant that you were a swimmer plastered in the discharge from a ship's tanks.

Raw sewage was also a problem, and the local Scuba clubs began to haul in some very unsavoury things indeed at the end of their spear-guns. Eventually, in 1992, the conservation organisation Greenpeace arranged a massive protest on Southend seafront. In order to highlight the problem of sewage discharge, they brought with them a very special prop, a giant inflatable, speckled plastic turd. They gambolled with this on the beach for the benefit of photographers, played a brief game of beach-volleyball with it, and then invited reporters to treat it as a boat. For seaworthiness, the plastic dungboat was a definite improvement on a great many vessels that I have sailed in.

In the long term, the protest certainly achieved its aim, which was to stop the sewage company pumping waste into the Estuary. The humble turd had proved a good deal more effectual than most politicians. It also produced an unexpected side-effect, a massive rise in the number of bathers and dippers making legal claims. Many of these claims were pretty bizarre. I telephone-interviewed one gentleman who claimed to have come out in giant yellow spots all over his body. "I went swimming and soon as I was out of the water, these big blotches started popping up all over. It's a pity you haven't got a video phone or I could show them to you," he said. Fortunately, a miracle cure took place overnight and by the time the photographer arrived next morning the blotches had gone. He had to be painted up with canary make-up to simulate the effect. "It was handy he had a pot of yellow make-up in his flat, to start with, really," mused the photographer.

A further unexpected result of all this negative publicity was that the number of swimmers in the Estuary actually *went up*. The suspicion dawned that many of them were actually hoping to contract something nasty, in the hope that they could then obtain compensation. Not for two centuries had the world descended in such droves on Southend to seek out its soothing waters. The difference was that on this occasion they were seeking, not to shake off, but to acquire, an illness. One man even claimed to have caught a venereal disease from swimming off Southend. Wags on the newsdesk swiftly dubbed him the "shark-shagger."

Eventually, an official scientific enquiry was held into the state of the Estuary water. I volunteered as a guinea-pig on behalf of the newspaper. Such was the reputation of the Estuary by now that I was provided with special insurance cover from a fund normally reserved for journalists covering dangerous sports, or reporting from Chechnya. That year, too, I noticed, absolutely nobody kissed me under the mistletoe at the office Christmas party.

The seawater did have one definite, palpable physical effect. Minutes after emerging from the water, I realised that part of me was missing. Had I, wonderful thought, lost a limb? If so, the headlines would be huge, and the smile on my family solicitor's face even bigger. Then I realised what had happened. My athlete's foot had disappeared. Just a few minutes before, the site conditions between my toes had been positively gory. The condition had been a long-lasting one. The threat: "The toe is coming to get you" was enough to get the most reluctant child scuttling upstairs to bed. My toes had been sprayed with enough chemicals to defoliate Vietnam, all to no avail. Now the Estuary saltwater had succeeded where the Swiss drug companies had resoundingly failed. Newspaper readers were duly regaled with more details than they probably really wanted to know about the process. The athletes responsible for this condition clearly weren't Olympian swimmers, and had never since made a reappearance. Six months later I was cross-questioned by government doctors, and the effects of Southend brine on one Essex body are now inscribed for all time in the health records of the nation.

Remembering this, I now removed my boots and socks and joined Essex Dog, who was already frolicking in the water. She was leaping up and down, all four legs rigid, apparently in an attempt to ambush a passing school of jellyfish. She, who had barely set eyes on the sea until a few weeks ago, had now taken to it with a passion that suggested she might have been a cat-fish in a former life. We sloshed our feet in the saltwater for a few minutes before returning up the beach to the concrete walkway. I had learnt one thing from being an Estuary guinea-pig. But as we set out for the long walk, the much-abused sea-water had another healthy effect – it had put us in sparkling good spirits. In my notebook, under the heading Future Business Projects, I jotted: "Open mental health sanatorium on beach. No barbecues."

Ahead of us stretched the undiscovered trail around the Estuary. It didn't actually look very undiscovered. It was swarm-ing with people and – despite notices banning them during the summer months – dogs. Well, that's dyslexic canines for you. Yet apart from a few casual strollers, nobody was actually trav-elling along the trail. For the picnickers and sunbathers, it rep-resented just a giant public patio. It did indeed appear that we were the first souls in history to recognise the esplanade's potential for a long-distance journey. As rather overdressed hikers, we in fact proved something of a novelty. We had visit-ed a car-boot sale to buy equipment for the walk, and I had come away with a British Rail trackworker's dayglo orange vest, easily spotted by any air ambulances looking for trade. I had also acquired an impressive rucksack, designed for Himalayan expeditions. Apparently intended to pack the expedition's HQ marquee in its ample depths, the rucksack was, truth to tell, somewhat underused by us. It carried a round of salami sand-wiches, my reporter's notebook, and some old broken ship's bis-cuits to sustain the dog. I had packed the rest of the space with old mackintoshes (like most reporters, I own an abundance of the things), since a sagging rucksack is possibly the world's sec-ond saddest sag after a punctured silicon implant.

We walked fast for the next two miles, despite the temptation to strike up conversation with the wild pleasure-seekers of the seafront, and although many of them clearly needed able-bodied help in pumping up their airbeds. We were brought up short, however, by a large noticeboard. "You are looking," it announced, "at England's largest nature reserve." Essex Dog and I looked around for tell-tale signs of pampas grass and wildebeest, but all we could see was the Estuary. Then it dawned on us: it was the Estuary that the noticeboard was talking about!

The Largest Nature Reserve in England! It would be good to report that, with this amazing revelation, the Estuary came alive, just as it had at that wedding all those years ago. The thing about a nature reserve is that it heaves with life, right? Yet the Estuary was just its usual self, full of rude human activity, but noticeably lacking in anything else very wild. Essex Dog was uninhibited, but that was a bit different. A few gulls were wafting over the waves, but frankly, if it was gulls you wanted to see, you'd be better off taking your binoculars to a rubbish tip, ten miles inland. Some pigeons, no doubt following the Thames on the way to Trafalgar Square, had paused just long enough to drop some dove-poo on the notice-board, but it was hard to imagine even the most besotted naturalist bothering to set up a nature reserve on their behalf. Apart from that, there was simply mud, sea and sky, things which even in these conservation-conscious days scarcely need to be protected from poachers.

We stared long and hard at the Estuary for any signs of animal-life. Even a little annual migration of, say, leaping lobsters, would have satisfied us. But the Estuary just lay there, frumpish and grey, like an elderly spinster having a little lie-down. How could this be a nature reserve at all, let alone the biggest in a nation that catered for beavers, leaping mountain-goats and whales, though not all in the same reserve of course.

Nor could I remember any official declaration. The Mayor hadn't cut any cord to declare the Estuary open to endangered species. Until now, the local press seemed to have missed the biggest thing to hit the Estuary since Nellie the forty-stone human mermaid regularly plunged into its waters a hundred years ago. Once again, the Estuary was demonstrating its talent for the unexpected.

We continued along the seafront. We passed two girls in what looked like Tudor tapestry bikinis, but all thoughts of people-watching or firing impertinent questions had gone now. Our eyes were for the Estuary alone, as we scanned that great wilderness of inert mud for anything with lips or beak. Even a limpet would have sufficed. I wasn't quite sure what a limpet looked like exactly, but I had some notion that it was some sort of secretive bowel system with flippers. It attached itself to surf-boards and then sucked in as much of them as it could without being noticed. But even the limpets were lying low.

The traffic and the crowds grew more intense. Before we knew it, we were at the Kursaal dome, one of the few landmarks on the Estuary. In its heyday as a seaside resort, Southend's motto had been: "By the Dome it's Known." The Dome front-ed a huge permanent fairground, complete with roller-coaster, water-splash and the famous Kursaal Flier, a full-size steam engine. Its founder and owner, CJ Morehouse, had spent his young manhood in the Wild West a hundred-odd years ago. He used to test some of the fiercer rides dressed in full cowboy buckskins and carrying a Winchester rifle and a Bowie knife in his teeth. "Wilder than a bucking Bronco" he would claim of his roller-coasters. It was meant to be a recommendation. The fairground was long ago built over, but the dome remains. It had just been beautifully and expensively restored. Now it housed a teashop, a bar and a lot of space that nobody quite knew what to do with. A few weeks before I had interviewed a petrified night-watchman. "The place is just wild with ghosts," he said. "The worst of them is this ghost with a stupid cowboy hat on, and he's got these terrible teeth."

"Terrible?" I asked. "What do you mean terrible? Are they canine teeth, or what."

"No, I mean, they need a lot of dental work done on them. They're all black and crooked. No wonder he moans so much."

At this stage I recalled Mr Morehouse's habit of carrying firearms in his mouth, which can't have helped his dental hygiene, particularly if the occasional pan-load of gunpowder went off by accident as he took a downward plunge on his roller-coaster. I wondered whether to look in at the Kursaal. But my appetite for the place and its ghosts had waned since seeing that notice-board on the seafront. The prime imperative now was to find out more about the Estuary as a nature reserve, and to see if there wasn't some way of going on safari in the mud. As I gazed over England's largest, not to mention most unassuming, nature reserve, I suddenly recalled to mind an oddly prophetic incident from a few years before. I'd been visited by an old friend, an American journalist who worked on the *St Louis Post Dispatch*, and his family. They had arrived in a flurry of anglophilia. Southend, though, had managed to dent this. They were puzzled by Kiss Me Quick hats, and false latex knockers were not the sort of thing they expected to see on sale. Not in a land that was supposed to be inhabited by Jeeveses and Woosters, while swarms of Mary Poppinses floated around on umbrellas keeping the skies respectable. Even worse, I introduced them to jellied eels. They ate the things with mounting disbelief. It was not long before they were ready to bomb Buckingham Palace. They would probably have thrown up there and then into the Estuary, except that I had just given them a long talk about pollution control.

Luckily, Southend pier worked its old magic, going some way to restore their enthusiasm for quintessential England. "It's the longest pier in the world," I announced. "One and a third miles long."

"You don't say. We could use something like that back home."

"What for?" I asked. "You live fifteen hundred miles from the sea."

"Who needs sea if you've got the longest pier in the world," said Charlie. "We'd stick it in a drive-thru. The longest sea-pier in the world? Geee! How many places can make a claim like that?"

"Not one," I said proudly. Weston-super-Mare had once tried to break Southend's record, by building an extension to their pier. But when they were just a few feet from achieving their aim, something blew the extension away. At the time, guerrilla action by the Southend Formation Swimming team was blamed. "But I reckon the reason was more straightforward," I told my American friends. "God was on Southend's side, simple as that."

We paid our tickets and began the long walk to the souvenir shops and games arcades, one and a third miles out to sea. As we walked, they read from an old Council guidebook to the pier. Somehow it had made its way to an antiquarian bookshop in the American Midwest, where Charlie had found it on a rainy Saturday afternoon. Now he'd brought it home again.

"It says here that it was built in order to disembark Londoners from paddle-ships," said Charlie.

"That's right," I told them. "Before the pier came, anyone who wanted to get ashore had to be carried over the mud on the back of a local fisherman."

Charlie peered over the parapet at the world of soggy caramel beneath the pier. "Guess they got a lot of spinsters coming on those trips, eh."

He was still up to making jokes at this stage. But his sense of humour, or humor as his spellchecker would call it, evaporated fast under what, he at any rate, viewed as the torment of a bracing English-style walk. We hadn't gone more than a few hundred yards before Charlie and Dandy started to become positively bilious, in stomach and in spirit. I had forgotten how puzzled Americans are by the idea of walking. Walking is something that escaped prisoners and illegal immigrants do. If God had meant us to walk along Southend pier, he would have given us wheels and vertebrae that lit up whenever we applied the brakes. Charlie and Dandy clearly regarded this pier walk as some weird English practical joke.

"It says here that Southend pier has a unique, self-contained railway system. Originally it was a horse-drawn tramway," said Charlie. "That sure sounds fun."

"I thought we could take the train back from the far end."

"I'm a bit of a train buff," said Charlie, in a sudden unexpected revelation. "Can't get enough of the things. I'd like to take the train out and back again."

"I thought you'd want to take a good look at the scenery."

Charlie and Dandy both peered at the mud. "Scenery?" he enquired.

"It gets better the further out you go," I said, rather lamely. "There's a good view back of the ... er ..." I glanced back, to where a long line of teak boards marked our progress. "Well, there's a good view of the pier itself."

We plodded on for a few hundred more yards. As exhaustion and aching joints set in, Charlie's most basic instincts were set into play. Charlie worked as an investigative reporter, so his most basic instinct is to fire probing questions. He started to cross-examine me as if I had been some dodgy senator from the Louisiana swamps.

"This pier thing," said Charlie. "What's it do. I mean, like, what's it for? You haven't got paddle-steamers any more."

"Well, it's living history," I said.

"What sort of history?"

"Well, for instance, in the Second World War, as your book will tell you, it joined the Navy. It was called *HMS Leigh* and it became the command centre for all East Coast operations. The Germans used to strafe it, so they mounted machine-guns on the pier trains."

"The war's over, buster," said Charlie. "Maybe the Germans had the right idea, trying to shoot the pier. So are you saying it's a sort of war memorial?

"Well, no."

"It must cost big bucks to run it."

"Yes."

"So, does anybody make any money out of it."

"Well, no. Lots of people lose money on it, though," I ventured hopefully.

"So why don't you just, you know, knock the thing down? There's some rednecks I know, got their own Sherman tanks, do it for you for the price of a beer."

"You wanted to import it to America a few minutes ago."

"Well, now I got close up to it and I guess I realise why we haven't got round to buying it," said Charlie, rubbing his kneecaps. "So what else good-for-something does your pier do?"

"Well, it offers a great walk. A healthy walk." The living disproof of that was in front of my eyes. Charlie and Dandy were becoming unhealthier by the yard.

The American looked at me in disbelief. "It's just another boardwalk," he said. "A boardwalk across mud. Dead mud."

There was something about that phrase, "dead mud", that stung past enduring. Every Essex man and woman loves Southend pier. Nobody questions what it's there for. It's obvious. It's there to be the longest and best pier in the world.

"It may be just dead mud," I told him. "But that is the *biggest* area of dead mud in northern Europe. There is enough dead mud out there to cover two cities the size of Manhattan, with even the helipads covered – yes, that muddy! As for the pier, it's the longest in the world and you're just sore because you haven't got it. It is 6,864 feet long; the Empire State Building is only 1,250 feet high. So once Southend Council gives itself planning permission to stick the pier on end, it will also be the world's tallest building."

Oddly enough, this blast of statistics seemed to mollify Charlie, even physically reinvigorate him. "The biggest area of dead mud in Europe. Phew! That's quite something, I'll give you that," he muttered. He stared out with renewed respect at the Estuary, and I didn't have the heart to tell him that I had plucked this particular muddy figure, the one about it being the largest area of mud in northern Europe, out of the air.

Yet here, a decade later, was official confirmation of my claim. The Estuary mud really was a statistical champion. Only the word "dead" was inaccurate. It wasn't the largest area of deceased mud in Europe, it was the largest area of living mud. It was so alive that it had a preservation order on it, presumably so that nobody harassed it during the mud-pie mating season.

Yet staring out over the mud on this sunny day, I could not, for the life of me, comprehend how that inert brown morass, where all the leftover Brown Windsor soup from all the minus one-star boarding houses in England went to die, could possibly be alive. Luckily, I knew a bughunting double-act who might be able to explain.

Laurence Watts and John Skinner, from the natural history department of the Southend Museum, are the Estuary's Baywatchers. I knew that, for years now, they had been compiling surveys of marine life in the Estuary. As I understood their method, they monitored catches from professional fishing-vessels on a systematic basis. They then reported their findings to the scientific journals, producing a precision record. All of which made me an interesting natural history study in my own right, as a rare example of homo-sapiens recently fallen out of a Christmas tree.

What Laurence and John actually do, it turns out, is wade out into the mud beneath Southend pier. They do so whenever they can get away from their duties at the museum identifying ladybirds brought in by schoolchildren. Out in the mud, they lift up stones, and set down their findings in a damp notebook. Laurence and John suggested that I come out with them on one of these mud forages. "You'll discover just how alive the Estuary is," said Laurence. "There's this little world – well, not so little world, really – that Laurence and I have observed, and not too many others."

I met with them at eight o'clock on a raw morning. Southend's answer to the Baywatch team were warmly dressed in anoraks, waterproof gloves and extra-long wellies, and they clutched weather-beaten buckets – possibly their proudest possessions – and long fishing nets. They looked, it has to be said, about as far removed from Pamela Anderson in a bikini as it is possible to get, while yet belonging to the same species. But there was no doubt that they meant business.

Today's lap of the Estuary walk was to be into the Estuary for a change, rather than alongside it. We followed the magnificent ironwork undercarriage of the pier, as it guided us through the domain of lugworm and mussel, out towards the shipping lanes. I had walked the length of the pier dozens of times, often dragging squawking, protesting visitors. But this was the first time that I had walked out to sea *underneath* the pier. Just what Charlie and Dandy would have said about *that* didn't bear thinking about. The two naturalists, on the other hand, saw things from a different perspective. "There aren't many places better for studying Life than Southend pier," John announced.

And he was right. We hadn't waded out for more than a few yards before the mud started to come alive. Anything less dead it would be hard to imagine. The mud was dead like the graduation concert at the Egomania Academy for the Performing Arts is modest and self-effacing. There and then I fingered the mobile, wondering whether to ring Charlie and Dandy in St Louis, Missouri, where it was two o'clock in the morning, to teach them a lesson about Estuary mud. No, that mud positively teemed with the life force, in a manner more associated with the seafront on a Saturday night than the Estuary on a windswept Monday morning.

The first discovery was significant – a fat oyster, clenching one of the iron pillars of the pier.

"That may look just like an oyster to you," said John. Actually, in my ignorance I'd thought it was just a rusty

Victorian rivet, and vaguely wondered how to prise it off for my antique junk collection. "But it's also a sort of symbol," John informed me. "It's an indication of the revival of the Estuary. Oysters are very fussy about any sort of pollution. They are a good litmus paper. And these are definitely on the increase in the Estuary." I looked at the oyster. Now that I could identify him for what he was, he came across as palpably healthy. He, at least, wasn't complaining that he'd come out in yellow spots. She (for this was a hermaphrodite oyster) wasn't ringing Cherie Blair to take on her compensation claim. No, he-she-it was just enjoying life in a way that only encrustations on Southend pier and Italian playboys know how.

I was all for interviewing the oyster there and then. A wise pair of naturalists like John and Laurence were bound to understand its body language. But a cry went up from Laurence (there were to be lots more of these cries as we proceeded out to sea). "Look at this!"

I squelched over to where Laurence was holding a tiny water-pistol. As I approached, he squirted me. Some kid had obviously dropped it off the pier. Then the water-pistol wriggled angrily. "It's a sea squirt," said Laurence. On closer inspection, the little organism looked like a cross between a baby slug and a sliver of seaweed. But its pumping capacity proved to be awesome. "They can process forty gallons of water an hour," Laurence said. The tiny creature had all the pumping power of a human heart. But they are also the Estuary's kidneys. Give them a break and they will cleanse and filter all the water the Thames, and we, can dump on them.

Laurence had now turned his attention to a large rock, half embedded in the silt. "I feel a good boulder coming on," he whooped. The two naturalists positively danced in their wellies to the new site. John stood poised with his net at the edge of the rock. With a practiced flourish, Laurence whipped his boulder up and away. John pounced with his net, scooping up everything that swam, crawled or slept off its breakfast under what, a second before, had been the sheltered accommodation of the rock.

The space between rock and mud offered an immediate snapshot of that "little big world" that John had talked about. There were crabs of varied shapes, sizes, colours and levels of courage ("We've identified eighteen species in our surveys, and the number's rising," John told me). There were some sex-mad prawns. There was a shanny, a tiny, ugly little fish, with a powerful set of miniature shark teeth, evolved to rasp barnacles and mussels off whatever perch they are bedded on, then rip them out of their shell. Although just the size of a thumbnail, it can and will give a man a bite he remembers for a long time to come. "Nice little specimen," said Laurence. Nice wasn't in fact the first word that came to mind. And next to this creature from miniaturised hell sat a being from paradise, albeit a worm.

Visually the Peacock Worm lives up to his name. Mentally he is probably rather smarter and more alert than his bird counterpart. He builds a flexible tube, about one foot long, using the Estuary silt mixed with his own worm-slime. The bottom of the tube is anchored in the mud, but it offers a hatchway into the shallows. The worm can pop the crown of his head up to take a look at the world outside his tube, and also, presumably, to be looked at. For your Peacock Worm is a lovely sight. Even on a dull day, that worm-crown seems to sparkle. It distils a range of Caribbean hues from the greys and browns of the Estuary. Everyone who paddles in the Estuary must tread on scores of these tails of paradise, without realising it. But the peacock worm is usually ready for the flat-footed splish-splash merchant. It can withdraw that remarkable crown in a trice, leaving just its dull, rubbery housing.

"You know, most of the time we're busy with the specimens. But every now and then I stop, take a deep breath, and contemplate the sheer wonder of it all," said Laurence. He could see that by now I, too, had been affected by Estuary Fever. I was giggling like a baby with a new toy, every time a new species turned up. Here was a discovery, to be sure. There really was a life force in the Estuary. Truly, the mud was alive. It was no longer a vague suspicion, it was a scientific fact. Mind you, just how enviable a life it was out here was a different matter.

"You have to leave all your preconceptions about life as you know it on land when you come out here," Laurence said. "Basically it's non-stop carnage out here. Everybody wants to eat everybody else. You learn very early on that you've got to separate the various species if you're going to take them home. Otherwise you leave the sea with lots of specimens, and you arrive back at the house with just a single, fat, one."

"It's not always the species you'd expect, either," added John.

"Now, if it's nightmares you want," said Laurence, warming to his theme, "consider this one here." He had just found a common starfish. This symbol of the British seaside was looking extremely humble, as if a display of extreme modesty might just prevent it becoming part of the souvenir trade. But this apparently pleasant animal disguised a foul culinary secret. "Basically, it engulfs its prey with its stomach, then sits back and digests it."

Another leg of Southend pier, another cry. Laurence and John introduced yet one more fascinating creature of their acquaintance. This was the pea crab. It was a tiny, translucent creature, so named because even a *petit pois* chucked overboard by the *commis* chef on some passing liner would be enough to brain it. But the pea crab has protection. "It spends its entire life inside the shell of a mussel," explained Laurence. "You could say it's the ultimate in sheltered existences. The host draws in water, and the pea-crab filters its food from that. It does no harm to the mussel. It does some good in fact. The pea-crab pays his rent by scraping algae off the mussel's gills."

A good working partnership is always a heart-warming sight, added to which the crab was like a living pendant from a charm bracelet. With its understandably secure outlook on life, it was quite happy to curl up its claws, snuggle down, and go to sleep in my hand.

Yet even this magical miniature crustacean couldn't quite settle the disturbance that had dug into me. Was the Estuary throbbing and bubbling with life, or was it really pulsating with death? The teeming society of creatures that I had seen was vigorous enough by any measure, but it wasn't into anything like principles or purpose, other than Eat Thy Neighbour. If the Estuary did have a message, it was beginning to look like a rather uncomfortable one.

Why should I care? The selfish but sensible attitude would be: so, I've got problems of my own. You think you've got something to whinge about, Mr Barnacle, just because you're being slowly digested alive and the predator's previous meal smells of rotten fish. Well, you try paying off a mortgage on negative equity if you want to know what real problems are. Things are a lot worse at sea, I tell you. Well, actually, I suppose that you already know that.

So why should I care? The answer came, with blinding obviousness. I was one of them. Essex Man and Estuary mollusc are like that together. The long family tree drawn up by my great aunt, who had a private income and nothing better to do, actually extended to a prehistoric sea-slug that had hauled itself up onto the beach, swapped its slime for fur, and evolved into an ape. I was amongst my own. I had come home. That explained my euphoria as I splashed through the shallows. And that was why I cared about all this carnage, and vaguely wondered how difficult it would be to introduce starfish and other savage predators to some food that wouldn't suffer, like, say, nut cutlets.

Yet perhaps the cosmic picture wasn't so bad after all. "Life in the Estuary is burgeoning," John had told me. "New species, more varieties. The Estuary is hauling itself up by its bootstraps." He'd indicated an oyster (one of his most common practices). "Look at him. He's just sitting there getting bigger all the time." At that stage, I remembered those 4,000-year-old

piles of oyster shells, deposited by men and women who probably thought of themselves as half-mollusc. Four millennia ago
our oyster friend here would have ended up in that pile of
shells. But now the people on land had found other concerns
than oyster gathering. By turning our backs on the Estuary, we
had blessed it with the most benign force any wilderness can
ask for: neglect. We had allowed it to get on with its life. Real
rain forests and oceans the world over might be subject to environmental degradation. But the Estuary was on the up. And
that oyster just sat there, getting bigger and healthier all the
time.

This mudflat world yielded a weird paradox. The more mas-
sacre, the more the variety and quantity of life. What was more,
the mightiest process of all in the Estuary seemed to be that of
birth. Laurence introduced me to a brand new phrase. He
seemed to repeat it every time he came across a baby specimen.
"He's just come out of the plankton."

I only recognised the notion of plankton in the vaguest
sense, as something you offer a whale if you want to keep on the
right side of it. Laurence explained it in richer detail. "Think of
it as a kind of soup. Lots of sea-creatures, thousands in fact,
deposit their eggs into this soup. And that's it, as far as they're
concerned. That is the extent of their parental responsibilities.
They go their own way. The plankton then takes on a sort of
parental life of its own. This soup drifts through the seas – the
word plankton comes from the Greek for 'wandering'. But all
the time, some of those eggs within the plankton find the environment they are passing through is to their taste. And for a lot
of them, that environment is the Thames Estuary."

Hours had passed. We had made our way as far as the deep
water, close to the end of the pier, and back again. We were just
a hundred yards or so from journey's end when I got round to
asking John and Laurence about the nature reserve.

"Is it true?" I said. "Is it really the largest in England."

"That's right," said John, "It's official."

"So who looks after it? Who funds it? Where's the manage-ment system? What are the qualifications for becoming a ranger? How much does it pay? What are the pensions like?"

Laurence and John looked at each other. Obviously all these things were new notions to them.

"Well, in an ideal world, the Estuary, I suppose, well, looks after itself," said John, hesitantly. "If we give it half a chance. It is an ecosystem, after all."

"Are there any wardens."

"That's us," said Laurence.

"Just you two! For the entire Thames Estuary?"

"We don't know of anybody else. Anyway, we're not really official as such. We just keep a watchful eye on it."

"Doesn't the responsibility frighten you?"

"The Estuary is pretty good at looking after itself if we give it half a chance," said John.

"But it's very important, isn't it. Isn't it a bit too important to be left to just two part-time guys?" Important? Had I really said that? About the Thames Estuary?!

"The thing about the Estuary," said John, clearly trying very hard *not* to sound like an important official in a gold braid uni-form, "the reason perhaps why it matters most of all, is that it is a breeding ground. Species raised in the Thames Estuary, like, say, its baby plaice, spread everywhere. It's a very important supplier of life across a significant area. Laurence and I can't make this happen. The Estuary itself is doing that. But right now, what we can do, is monitor the improvements, and per-haps help people to understand what is going on."

"And you two are the only ones monitoring it."

"We do what we can," said John.

There they stood, the eyes, ears and guardians of the Estuary, two underfunded – no, unfunded – local museum cura-tors, their resources limited to a bucket and a net, plus an enthusiasm so boundless that it was more epidemic than infec-tious. They were kings of the Thames siltlands, if only because they knew its ways like no others. But they didn't particularly want to preside alone. They wanted to share this marvellous secret with anyone who would listen, anyone who was prepared to learn the extraordinary lessons.

And among those they had instructed had been me. I knew with absolute certainty now, how wrong the idea of "dead mud" is and always was. It would be impossible ever again to look out over a low tide and believe that life had receded with the water. The mudflats were no longer a desert of lifeless minerals. I had been taught now that tens of millions of births, meals and violent deaths were taking place in the huge muddy haven that was home to the wandering plankton and so much else, alongside the Estuary path, as we walked. No wonder the Estuary had been so neglected. It was that bane of all right-thinking journalists. It was a good news story.

The Gravesend statue of Queen Victoria, minus her right hand

The Southend statue of an older Queen Victoria, also missing her right hand

Six

Leigh, Hadleigh – and lost

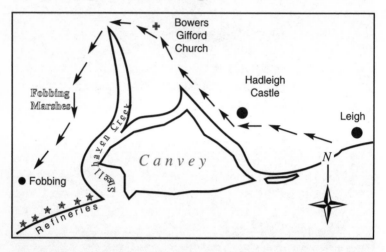

FOR the two and a half mile stretch from Leigh to South Benfleet, the Estuary trail does something altogether surprising. It becomes picturesque. In short order, it offers the mellowing Victoriana of Westcliff, a chocolate-box fishing village; an ancient, and memory-haunted castle; one of the most elegant seaside communities in Britain; and a pristine landscape of woods and turfy downs that come rolling down to the water's edge.

So it goes without saying that in the 1960s strenuous efforts were made to drive a six-lane motorway through this entire stretch of waterfront, demolishing the entire village of Old Leigh and much of the castle in the process. Forty years on, the project seems crazed – a typical piece of planning from the age that gave us the concrete jungle. Yet there were times when, up to my knees in mud and impatient with the slow pace of the trail, I actually started to doodle a six-lane highway onto the map of the Estuary, in a wistful sort of way. "It would be sort of nice to be bowling along the seafront in a heated coach," I told

Essex Dog. The dog, who was 75 years old in doggy years at the time, and would have qualified for one of Saga's tours, looked like she agreed.

The motorway went the way of other '60s wheezes, like the Skinnies pop group or snakeskin vests, but disappointed motorists are still free to *walk* along the route, muttering "brroomm, brroomm" if that helps. This delectable stretch of the trail begins with a dilemma. Where the Southend suburb of Chalkwell turns into the not-quite-Southend suburb of Leigh, a walker is spoilt for choice. He can follow a path along the edge of the sea. Or he can haul himself 95 feet above Mean Sea Level. Assuming his heart survives the effort, he can then beat a trail through the lofty greensward of Cliff Gardens. The two walks are in total contrast. The sea-level path takes you alongside a bustling, workaday waterway, full of busy fishermen and yachtsmen with terrible colds, who've rung in sick to the office so that they can spend the day varnishing their boats. Climb to the gardens, on the other hand, and these prosaic waters are suddenly transformed. The whole of the Estuary is spread in front of you, full of magic, mystery and far away places. In the unlikely event that this view palls, there is an alternative gawp in the shape of the sumptuous properties skirting Cliff Gardens. These are the most expensive residences to be found anywhere on the Thames Estuary, give or take the odd luxury yacht slumming it for the night in a tidewater creek. It is a perfect spot in every way, at least for those who like scenery. Swinging types may find it a touch quiet and conservative. Certainly a nice motorway would have helped to give it that touch of jazz it lacks.

You pays your money – in the case of the cliff houses, without getting much change from a million – and you takes your choice. But the decision was too fraught for us. So we compromised. We walked both routes. We followed the seafront path from Chalkwell station to Old Leigh, then swung up the cliff. Well, it would be fairer to say that we shuffled up. I was weighed down by a bulky volume of paintings that I was carrying in my knapsack, *Essential Constable*. Not only was it a dead weight, but its corners also had a habit of digging into the small of my back however carefully I adjusted it. I finally settled the book's hash by wrapping the dog's swimming towel round it, a terrible fate for anything in creation, but cruelly necessary under the circumstances. At last we reached the top of the hill.

We paused, for old time's sake, outside Oscars, the function rooms. Then we retraced the route, heading east through the Cliff Gardens. Human interest then proved more compelling than scenery, so we repeated our trail along the waterfront to see if any of the yachtsmen had succumbed to varnish poisoning. Thus, after a circle and a half, we finally arrived at Old Leigh High Street.

Leigh is a multi-textured community. Its northern territory is a sprawl, clustered round the old coaching road – now the A13. It has one unique claim to distinction. In the 1920s and 1930s, this stretch of road evolved into the nation's second-hand car capital. "You'd get real toffs, Mayfair quality types, turn up there to look for cars," one old dealer recalled. "They'd often find what they wanted too. What do you think that was, old son?"

"A nice cheap motor," I suggested.

"No," he chortled. "Cars that had been nicked from them in town the week before."

The centre of Leigh is an area of wide roads and prosperous lives. The Jewish community is large enough for the area to have been dubbed Golders Green-on-Sea, at least in pre-politically correct days. Local hostelries advertise: "Weddings and bar mitzvahs catered for."

Whichever part of Leigh they live in, most people identify the town by its third level, the old fishing village. This consists of what, being the lowest street around, is humorously called the High Street, a medieval alleyway fronted by ancient cottages. From here, a steep set of pedestrian steps mounts to the old church on top of the hill. Further rows of fishermen's cottages are perched precariously alongside these steps. Modern houses and flats hustle Old Leigh on all sides, yet the tiny village somehow keeps its sense of intactness. The harbour is cosy and protected. The sea laps the very edge of the high street. It has flourished as a fishing haven since the dawn of tartare sauce. In the middle ages, its oysters were so renowned that scurvy fishermen from the Kent side of the Estuary actually launched armed raids on the oyster-beds. The whole place is reminiscent of a Cornish fishing village. Also in common with Cornwell, Leigh has a vociferous independence movement.

One factor, perhaps the only one, that unites all three levels of Leigh, is an unwillingness to be referred to as part of Southend. "Leigh was here 1,000 years ago, before Southend even had a name," Leigh people will tell you with gritted teeth and clenched fist. At this point, it is best to leave town, whatever name you choose to call it.

The different particles that make up Leigh – or West Southend as those who like to live dangerously put it – all seemed to merge together in one of the most bizarre stories that I ever covered for a local newspaper. The location was Oscars, the dining suite appropriately perched between the old fishing village and the new town.

A new husband and wife management team had just moved into the function room. Within a few days of their arrival, they rang the newsdesk to report a ghost sighting. Within days, the paper had published a picture of the ghost. Was it horrifying? Was it grisly! Did it bear a bloodcurdling resemblance to a junior reporter in a bath-robe, double exposed on the negative? Yes, yes, oh yes again.

So far, so routine. However, at this stage, enter Crystalbelle (not her real name, which was more outlandish), the séance specialist. "I realise that the so-called ghost photograph is a pack of codswallop," she told me on the phone. "But however much trouble you seek to have at their expense, I have to tell you that the people at those function rooms are genuinely disturbed by a presence. What they need is a nice good exorcism. I can give it to them, and if you choose to sit in on the occasion, perhaps it may relieve you and other members of your profession of some of your cynicism in these matters."

"I find that sort of talk very hurtful," I said. "Do you need an accomplice? We've got a nice youth opportunities kid here if you need to do any sacrifices."

Crystalbelle turned out to be a card, a gravel-voiced, chain-smoker with an extraordinary taste in gin and home-made wine. She was in constant communication with the other sort of spirit world as well. Her skills ranged across the whole gamut of spiritualist, from communication with the dear-departed to healing. She was particularly adept at astral travel, which she used as a handy device to check out her holiday accommodation. She had just arranged a holiday for herself and her (in-house wine-making) husband, in the Canary Islands. Before she clinched the booking, her spirit self had flitted over to the Canaries to check out that the linen in the rooms was clean and the food didn't have too much of that foreign garlic stuff in it.

The managers at Oscars agreed to allow us to publicise the exorcism. Not only did they feel that all publicity is good publicity, but they also felt that the chance to put a message like: "Cleared of ghosts" on their menus would help drum up trade. So it was that one dank afternoon, just as the light was falling, we convened at Oscars for tea and exorcism.

"Yes, there's definitely some disturbed vibrations here, my dears," said Crystalbelle, as we entered the main function room. "Just a moment while I consult Black Wolf of the Wind."

"Who?"

"My Spirit Guide. I'm surprised you can't see him. His feathers are taking up half the room."

"What is he?" the photographer asked. "A dead parrot?"

"He's a Red Indian chief. He's always with me. He was a

great warrior when he was alive. He took eighty scalps and wiped out an entire Spanish settlement."

"What's he doing in Leigh-on-Sea, then?" I asked.

"Oh, he comes here for the peace and quiet," said Crystalbelle, without a trace of irony. After a few seconds with her head cocked on one side, and her hearing-aid pivoted in the invisible Black Wolf's direction, a smile spread over her features.

"Black Wolf tells me that he has met the lady who is the cause of the little difficulty. She is a bit shy. She is hiding in the shadows in the corner over there."

"She probably doesn't want to be scalped," muttered the photographer.

"I don't think a full exorcism is going to be necessary after all," said Crystalbelle. "Just a quiet chat with her should do the trick. Now, my dear. There's no need to be afraid. Let's take a look at you. What do you make of her, Black Wolf?"

Black Wolf yelled something inaudible into her ear. "He says he's not very good at costumes," Crystalbelle explained. "Deer-slaying is more his line, but he thinks she's wearing a Gamages dress from the 1920s." There was another pause while Crystalbelle pointed her hearing-aid towards the corner of the room where the poor ghost was cringing. "Ah, now we're getting somewhere," she said. "Gently with her now, Black Wolf. Don't poke your tomahawk up her nose. She'll be much more forthcoming if you treat her kindly."

Crystalbelle moved into the corner of the room, and then made a great show of intent listening. "Right, I think we're there," she said, at last. "I haven't managed to get her name yet, but she was killed in the street outside. She was hit by a fat man with a big moustache, rosy cheeks and a loud voice in a big motor-car with three wheels. She says she doesn't know much about cars but even she knows that they're supposed to have four. She's still a bit shaken up by the experience, but I think … Oh no, what's this?"

Crystalbelle's voice suddenly changed. It acquired what might pass for a manly tenor, and burst into song. I was so surprised by this unexpected turn-up that I only managed to catch a few of the lines. Pieced together in retrospect from my notebook, however, this was the gist of the ditty:

I am a simple fisherman,
Of fair and famous Leigh,
And when I wish to wet my nets,
Why then I put to sea.

CHORUS: With a sack of sprats, and two drowned rats,
We're happy as can be
Add a bully crab, a plaice, a dab
And that shall be our tea,
When we sail back home to Leigh.

Crystalbelle's eyes had been shut throughout this rendition. At the end of the song, they opened again. She slumped against the wall, and looked exhausted. "Did what I think happened, happen?" she asked.

"You sang a song. Something about a fisherman."

"Bugger it," she said. "That always happens when I do a session in one of these old taverns. Lots of other spirits think there's some sort of party going on and try to muscle in on the act. Give it a break boys. Oh no, who's this."

Crystalbelle's eyelids dipped and she started to intone again. The words were thick, fast and obscure. Again, I could only take down odd shorthand fragments. But the gist of them soon became clear. Crystalbelle's eyes flicked open again. "I think I know what that was. 'Ya amod barmitzvah bereb." Am I right?"

"Er, yeah, I think it was something like that."

"This place must have played host to bar mitzvahs at some stage. All the sonorities of the place are getting into my head. I'm becoming so confused. All those voices jumbling together."

She closed her eyes and began to sing again, and this time I did succeed in taking down the bulk of her song.

I am a Jewish fisher lad,
Of fair and famous Leigh,
And when I sail back into port,
Bar Mitzvahed I shall be.

CHORUS: With a codfish jaw and half an oar,
Mussel-toff to you and me,
Grab some caviar and tabboulehya
And we're kosher as can be,
When we sail back home to Leigh.

Crystalbelle's eyes opened once again. She looked around her blankly. "What was I singing?" she asked.

"I don't know," said the photographer. "But whatever it was, I don't think it's going to make the charts."

Crystalbelle stared around her. "She's gone. What's happened to her, Black Wolf. Uh-huh. Uh-huh. Black Wolf says she's gone and won't be coming back." Crystalbelle beamed the beam of someone who is proud of her afternoon's work. "Well, it looks as if we won't have to go through an exorcism after all," she told the proprietors. "I don't think that you'll be troubled any further. You haven't got a double gin somewhere behind that bar by any chance, have you?"

Crystalbelle was as good as her word, and we heard no further word from Oscars. The poor spirit of the girl squashed outside Oscars all those years ago clearly could not take the mayhem, and had departed for other, quieter haunts. Or, depending on your convictions, you could just dismiss the entire exercise as yet another scheme by Crystalbelle to land herself an afternoon's worth of free gin. Only now, many years later, did I see it from another angle. We might not have witnessed a genuine exorcism, but we had been granted an impromptu pageant of the history of Leigh. The canny spirits knew in advance that this trip was going to happen, and had helped out as best they could with a bit of potted history. All the elements were there, from the fisher-folk who had originally created the place, through dodgy motor cars and Jewish cultural and social life. It was an odd, but oddly accurate, history lesson. All Leigh history was there, wrapped up in a psychic's babble.

Nowadays there is a fourth stratum to Leigh's history. I had hoped to sit in on the central steering committee for the Independent Leigh movement, but she was on holiday on the day I walked through the village. Instead, I met Lynn Tait, the nostalgia tycoon. We sat in the saloon of the Peter Boat, an old smugglers' inn (but then, most waterside pubs are; the novelty of a sign that read: "No smugglers slept here" would probably attract a roaring trade). We looked out at the crowds in the beer-garden, munching their way through cockles, mussels, whelks and jellied eels, and we talked about nostalgia, the industry of the future.

Just a few years ago, Lynn Tait was an unambitious primary school teacher, with an interest in vintage picture post-cards. Then she assembled a few items from her old Southend collection into a calendar, sold them for charity, and an industry was born. She now employs eight artists, has won numerous business awards, and her nostalgia gift shop in Old Leigh High Street is the largest concern in town. "Just every now and then I marvel at the pace with which it's all happened," she told me. She added, ever the professional nostalgia merchant: "It makes me quite wistful for the simple days when I was just a mum."

Leigh is the only olde worlde village on the entire Estuary. As a result, it is subject to flood-tides – not marine ones but human. On high days and holidays, the village is crammed with trippers, while the few genuine fisher folk left in the village cower behind their nets, or on the Algarve. What the visitors are buying into is tradition. Hence the hungry folk from Dulwich, sampling whelks with the remark: "You're sort of biting your way into Edwardiana, aren't you?" Hence the throngs in Lynn Tait's emporium.

But there is no need to grieve for some lost past when you head out of Leigh village and onto the Benfleet Downs. The world here belongs to all three tenses. It is now as it always has been on the hills. The Victorian railway is the only intruder on a timeless, protected landscape. The most confirmed old codger would be hard put to mutter: "If only it was like it was 10,000 years ago, when I was a lad," because it still is.

A field-path makes a beeline for Hadleigh Castle, rising gently up a broad, grassy ramp, known as the Saddleback, to the castle's eastern turrets. It was a glorious ascent, on a still afternoon. The only fly in the ointment was my copy of *Essential Constable*. The book had succeeded in casting off the dog's towel, and was now practising its diploma course in acupuncture on my back with renewed vigour.

Once within the Castle walls, the dog started howling (thirteenth century, yuck!). While she whinged across the Estuary, I threw down the rucksack, threw myself down on the grass within the castle keep, and extracted my tormentor – *Essential Constable*, its corners now blunted from all that jabbing. Before consulting it, though, I took a good look around.

Hadleigh Castle is the ruin of a ruin, yet it is still magnificent. I had visited it many times, sometimes staging stories here, but always by car. Today I had walked and sweated for the view, and it was like seeing it for the first time. Short of being catapulted in astride a boulder from a siege engine, there could be no better way to arrive.

It sits on the highest point in the Estuary, and few fortresses anywhere command a wider horizon. There are 295 square miles of tidal river within view, every square inch a potential troublemaker. Hadleigh is, or was, the Estuary's watchtower. Its role was more that of police constable than soldier. It spent more time eyeing up fishermen, cod, and other untrustworthy types than defending the realm. Its creator, Hubert de Burgh, was an ambitious courtier, as, or more, interested in impressing the natives than in frightening Frenchmen.

Whole books have been written about other castles. With Hadleigh, there are really only three things to say – enough to fit out a respectable paragraph or two. For all Hadleigh Castle's magnificence, some bungalows command more comment.

The first and most obvious point about Hadleigh Castle is its situation. If there is a better spot for picnics or seductions in southern England, any number of ageing types in cravats and 1950s sports cars would love to know it. Of all the places on the Estuary trail, this is the hardest to leave. Perhaps the advice to walkers should be: keep on moving. Don't let the enchantress beguile you with the view, or you'll leave the place, if at all, with lead hiking-boots.

The second point to make is that nothing, absolutely nothing, has ever happened here. Hadleigh Castle was fading almost as soon as it was constructed, around 1220. Just twenty years later, the Sheriff of Essex reported sniffily (he had a very well-kept castle of his own) that the place was falling down. There was one brief period of restoration and extension work during the reign of Edward III (1327-77). With that exception, Hadleigh Castle has been crumbling every since. The act of collapsing has been the nearest thing to violent activity that Hadleigh has ever known. It was almost as if it was built to be a ruin. Every now and then, a section of Hadleigh's curtain-wall or a turret or two would roll down the hillside. Possibly a few locals were mown down by these moving walls. If so, it was the most aggressive action ever to emanate from these peaceable quarters. As for human drama, Hadleigh has witnessed a riot of melodrama, murder, farce and comedy. But this has all been confined to the open-air theatrical productions and pageants held within its walls. The real-life medieval inhabitants seem to have spent their time cultivating vegetables in the castle gardens, angling in the fishponds, and – then as now – gazing at the view.

There are castles – the Tower of London or Corfe Castle for instance – that set the heart pounding, just through thinking about their stirring and bloody history. By way of contrast, there are also the herbivorous castles. One look at them is enough to reduce blood pressure that has been stirred up elsewhere, by overwork, office politics, or thinking too hard about the history of the Tower of London. Hadleigh belongs resoundingly in this category. The placid castle, so free of ghosts or bad memories or indeed memories of any sort, is balm for the spirit.

Hadleigh Castle's serenity has the ultimate stamp of approval. It was painted by John Constable, most familiar of landscape artists. You can't get any higher in the placid rankings than that. Constable's canvases of Essex rivers, fields and skies are reproduced all over the world. Indonesians put them on table-mats. Lumberjacks in the frozen north stitch embroidery samplers of The Haywain in order to get in touch with their feminine side. Arizona motel-owners hang two-tone copies of Flatford Mill on the walls of their bedrooms because Constable is out of copyright. I have even read that Constable's pictures hang in the surgeries of those psychiatrists who deal with mad-dog serial killers, although I never got close enough to one to check this out.

So if Constable paints a view, it is, by definition, tranquil. And John Constable went out of his way to paint Hadleigh Castle, taking an uncomfortable coach-ride to a place that was just as unfashionable in 1832 as it is now. It was good to know that the most famous English painter also shared a taste for the Thames Estuary, even if his paintings did keep stabbing me in the back. Now at last *Essential Constable* was going to justify its presence in my rucksack. What more halcyon way to pass an hour or so, than by sitting on the grass inside Hadleigh Castle, looking at the view, and then looking at Constable's rendition of it? This meditative rhythm would only be interrupted as I hurled the occasional lump of battlement at any chatty passer-by who interrupted these reveries.

So I settled down, found the pages about Hadleigh Castle, and got ready for a massive dose of karma. But the tranquillity didn't flow at all. Quite the opposite. What a shock! The landscape in Constable's picture was a place of violent skies, shattered land, a desolate, almost post-Armageddon world where carrion birds hovered for the few remaining pickings. Hadleigh lowered over this hellscape, a castle of the dead captured in dislocated brush-strokes. I thumbed back a few pages, to make sure that I hadn't picked up *The Bumper Book of Psychopaths' Remedial Paintings* in error. But no, here were the familiar, consoling paintings of barges, rivers, horses and windmills, all marching in company between the same covers as that demonic vision. I looked up at the real view. It was recognisably the source of this painting. The only change since Constable's day lay in the loss of one or two turrets from the castle, possibly even demolished by Constable in his rage, and the trains that occasionally rattled past on the marshes below. What had this gentle spot done to gall Mr Constable, normally the living embodiment of the "hallo birds, hallo butterflies, hallo pretty baglady" school of laid-back philosophy? So much so that his painting had turned this beauty-spot into a depiction of the bus-station to hell?

The answer, as it happened, lay within the covers of *Essential Constable* itself. Just for once I didn't even have to ring anybody. On this occasion, a few lines of text spoke louder than any picture. The facts were plain, and overwhelmingly sad. The artist painted Hadleigh Castle in the immediate aftermath of his wife's death. They had courted one another for twelve long years of buttoned-up passion. But his determination to earn his living as a painter, and his resulting penury, not to mention lack of respectability, prevented their marriage. At last Constable became established enough to achieve that ultimate artistic accolade, a mortgage, and Maria became Mrs Constable, the barge-painter's wife. But not for long. She died from a fever in 1832.

So Hadleigh Castle's greatest claim to fame is this: it was turned into a nightmare vision by England's most famous painter in the agony and rage of grief. There is a before and after with this place. You either know this fact, or you don't. Once you do become aware of the bitter artistic scenario enacted on this hillside, it is hard to go on thinking of the castle as a placid place – or to maintain that nothing ever happened at Hadleigh.

It certainly cast a mood of melancholy over what had, until now, been quite a cheery ambulatory jape. This atmosphere was enhanced by the Essex Dog's howling and whining. As her baying echoed across the Estuary, I imagined Kentish folk shaking their heads and muttering: "There's coyote in them thair hills; it's a sad old place, is Hadleigh." They didn't know the half of it.

Sad Hadleigh set the mood for the next stage of the Estuary Walk, which was to be shadowed by failure, frustration, and feuding.

The downland is a small, sweet aberration in the landscape, and the hills soon descend to marshland again, descending precipitately to South Benfleet. This consists of two ancient pubs, an ancient church, all backed by about 10,000 commuters, one of whom was Bing Crosby's last record producer. There is also an eating house where two French food journalists, here to write about the revival of English cuisine, were presented with a plate of Bird's custard trifle and some warmed-up potato crisps.

At Benfleet, for the first time, we actually left the edge of the Thames. We reluctantly skirted the passionate little island of Canvey. As editor of *Canvey Life* magazine – probably the high-point of my career – I had walked the fourteen-mile circumference of the island and knew that it demanded a book to itself. Canvey's west edge is cut off from the shoreline by Shellhaven Creek. This huge deepwater anchorage cuts three miles inland before petering out rather ignominiously in a south

Basildon timber-yard. As trailblazers, the dog and I had to find our way round this, before continuing along Thames shores.

But then, on the immediate far side of Shellhaven there lay an even more formidable obstacle, in the shape of the Coryton oil refineries. These stretch for four miles along the Estuary, and are one of the reasons why the Estuary has such a bad name amongst beauticians. It is certainly hard to imagine John Constable accepting a commission to paint these refineries, however desperate he was to pay off his mortgage. The terminals are, to use up my pun allowance, almost terminally ugly. There are times, it is true, when they do reveal a certain visual magnificence, when burning off gases in their giant Bunsen burners at night, or reflected in the creek in an evening light, or if your car has just run out of gas on the marshes. But they do hog a giant slice of the Estuary shore, while their chimneys dominate much of the landscape. And now they have made the shoreline inaccessible.

A trail used to run along the waterfront, but it was summarily closed off in the 1970s. Just for once, not a single rambler roared in protest. The argument for closure was undeniable. The IRA had just attempted to blow up the entire plant. Fortunately, the bomb failed to ignite. Newspapers at the time reckoned that, but for a faulty timing-device, flash explosions would have taken out the entire four miles of plant, and hundreds of lives. Much of the UK population would also have had to revert to pogo sticks for transport. As for the path between the river and the refineries, that still lies there, embalmed and overgrown, another casualty of the Irish troubles.

We could have requested special permission to walk the path. The plant managers owed me a favour, ever since I had once spent half an afternoon at a business seminar trying to find a story out of Statutory Amendments to secondary refining processes. But I had walked this path many years before, when Essex Dog was just a glint in the eye of a sex-mad whippet lurking behind a privet bush. Knowing what it was like, I wasn't in a hurry to walk it again. I remembered neat patterns of stainless steel pipes, chain-link fencing, cooling-towers, and some bouncing aardvarks. On reflection, I decided that I must have made up the aardvarks in my imagination, to relieve the extraordinary tedium of the walk.

Instead, we concocted a beautiful route across the Fobbing Marshes. I knew this stretch of marshland of old. I had once crossed it north to south following the track of a disused narrow-gauge railway, the Kinnochtown. In World War I the little toy trains of the Kinnochtown carried workers to the munitions factories by the river. The marshes acted as a blast zone. If the munitions plant blew up, the only casualties would be larks, and a few healthy cows. The munitions factories have gone, although of course the larks are more endangered than ever, and the cows a good deal less healthy. Although we would be leaving the river's edge, we would retain a clear view of the Estuary. The marshland between Fobbing and Benfleet is part of the Thames flood-plain. Remove the dykes and the river would reclaim this stretch of land instantly. Global warming being what it is, there was a good chance that would happen while we were rambling there.

That was the theory. Reality set in about one mile beyond Benfleet. It took the form of an elderly but determined lady, her arms akimbo, announcing: "You can't come this way." Essex Dog, who recognises real trouble as against posturing, suddenly evaporated from the landscape. I could hear her quaking in a hidey-hole by a drainage ditch.

"It's a footpath," I said.

"No it isn't. There's no footpath here. This is private land."

We squared up to one another. She was a fresh-faced person in, I judged, her early seventies. I looked the lady up and down to see if I could spot the tell-tale bulge of concealed monkey-wrench or, worse still, fence-pliers. No, she wasn't tooled up, although her body language beamed the message: *Centurion tank blocking path*. Emboldened by her lack of hardware, I asked:

"Who are you?"

"We farm here," she said. "Been here since the war, and I can tell you, there's no footpath here and never has been. My husband has been to court to decide that."

Headlines were already forming in my head. Here was a classic confrontation between downtrodden peasant, moi, and ruthless capitalist landlady. Even as we squared up, I was writing the story. "All we sought was to air our work-weary bones in the lush pastures of the Thameside meadows. Now, opposing our simple and humble needs, the sneering aristocrat stood blocking our path. With a cry of: 'Remove yourself from my vast estates,' she raised her riding crop to strike. But we too had a blow to strike – for the cause of freedom and the right of humble folk to roam the English countryside. With one bound I soared over Madam's shoulder and struck out on the path – the path of freedom – my faithful hound lolloping at my Achilles tendon."

Then I looked at the calmly determined little old lady confronting me. And I realised that there was a quite different way of interpreting the situation. I imagined the headlines in our rival newspaper, which never lost a chance to take a swipe:

Thug rambler, feckless cur, sought by police
Hack pushes old lady into drainage ditch

So instead I just said, rather pathetically: "But it's the only path there is across these marshes."

"I can't help that," she said. "There used to be paths here that'd give you a good walk, but nobody used them and then the rubbish tip covered some of them up. But be that as it may, there's no path through this farm."

"Very well, then," I said, "but you've not heard the last of this." I was well aware that crusading heroes didn't talk this way, except perhaps in real life. But the Estuary walk was having an effect. I was losing my taste for confrontational stories and gaining a taste for the peaceful life. I wanted to get on with the human race, even if it meant having to walk three extra miles to avoid them.

I turned round, in full scale retreat, and at that point the old lady said: "Wait a moment. I recognise you. You does that writing for the newspapers, don't you."

"Er, yes …"

"We read your stuff. You'd better have a cup of tea and meet my husband." She looked at my face. "You don't look a very happy hiker," she added, compassionately.

The lady, who we will call Mrs Snow, led me into the farmhouse where her husband was sitting. The farmhouse was pleasant enough. But it was hardly the haunt of a pair of peasant-manglers.

"Here's a turn-up," announced Mrs Snow. "It's that man that writes for the newspaper."

"Pleased to meet you," said Farmer Snow. "I read that stuff in that newspaper of yours, but I still can't let you walk across my land. We've been on this here marsh since 1952, and as I stand here before you, may I be cursed if I tell a lie, there has never been any footpath here. I know that for a fact, but I've still had to spend £8,000 in court to prove it. Now, have a cup of tea instead."

"Do you get many other walkers trying to come through?" I asked.

"Oh yes," said Mrs Snow. "They can get quite nasty. One of them frightened my cow. She was upset all afternoon." Mrs Snow was almost in tears at the recollection. But then she folded her arms in that determined fashion I was coming to recognise, and said: "But even so, he didn't come through."

I suddenly remembered something about this stretch of country. It was the sight of the Essex Footpath Murder.

Murder! The Italians commit it for politics, the French do it for love, the Americans do it for money, the Spanish do it for wounded pride and Eskimo women do it because their husband nicked the blanket. But only the English commit murder for country footpaths.

It happened on the banks of Shellhaven Creek, in 1832, just a mile or so from where we were taking tea. Captain Moir, the foul-tempered landowner, had shot a Barking man, William Malcolm, for walking along the ancient right of way by the creek. Captain Moir was hanged outside Chelmsford Assizes for his crime, a permanent warning to all those numerous people who might feel like taking a pot-shot at a passing rambler. Still, that didn't do poor William Malcolm much good, and now, in the same neighbourhood, we had Farmer and Mrs Snow, prepared to go to who-knew-what lengths to keep ramblers at bay. This wasn't the place or time to take a stand. So I drank tea, and talked cows, while Essex Dog eyed up the farm-dog talent.

To this day there is a gap in the Estuary trail, created by the Snow Farm. The Dog and I navigated round it by walking alongside the main Canvey Island road. We were in a low frame of mind. Our despondency wasn't even alleviated when a salesman from the newspaper passed by in his fancy motor and almost drove off the causeway waving at us. I looked up at the Benfleet Hills, which also appeared depressed. Who could blame them? They had been slagged off in a Constable canvas. It would have been good to spare some sympathy. It was just too bad about Constable's wife. But we all had our problems, and mine right now was a hole in my trail.

A few days later I contacted the council footpath officer, Terry Buck. Was there or was there not a path through the farm? And had he or had he not tried Mrs Snow's scones? "I'm afraid you've landed on the one path in the district that's in a state of limbo," Terry told me. "We say there is a path and Mr and Mrs Snow say there isn't. But they're an elderly couple living on their own in a remote place, and we don't want to seem to be bullying them. So at the moment there is a state of stalemate. As for the scones, I think I might have had one thrown at me. I'm not sure."

Stalemate was not how I would have described the situation, more a case of one determined pensioner with her arms akimbo, achieving outright victory. Those projecting elbows bisect the Estuary Trail as surely as any Hadrian's Wall. Still, it is worth a trip to that farm, just for the sight of Mrs Snow standing guard, keeping the world's pedestrians at bay, even though you'll get no further.

The walk improved for a while after this. We followed the railway line below Vange Hill, a doll's-house hill, proudly, but only just keeping its head out of the marshes, and seeming much grander than it really is by contrast with the giant billiard table that surrounds it. At the foot of Vange Hill, the path passes between the gravestones clustered around "the eel-catchers' church". St Margaret's, Bowers Gifford, is a small church built for a scattered marshland population. These were people who sometimes had to resort to stilts in order to wade to church on time.

If there is a more remote and hidden church anywhere within reach of Thames waters, it has probably been lost altogether by its bishop. Yet this isolated little outpost of the angels remains an active centre of local life. There are regular services, frequent weddings and – that great sign of vibrant life in any church – regular funerals. Brides and bridegrooms who can find their way to this isolated spot really do want to get hitched. Little, and little-known as it is, I find that Bowers Gifford church looms larger, as well as brighter, in the memory than Hadleigh Castle. Ten minutes around St Margaret's church was enough to top up the tanks with peace and light. As it happened, I was going to need all the reserves of these things to be found.

One mile beyond St Margaret's church is Pitsea Mount. Yes that's right, *mount*. Pitsea has been celebrated for its sense of humour since some warped tribal chieftain gave it such an enticing name. Like Vange Hill, Pitsea Mount seems higher than it really is, by contrast to the Thames flood basin into which it dips its feet, and it has an exaggeratedly grand name to match, redolent of sherpas and yetis. Another church – St Michael – stands at the top of Pitsea Mount. The two churches flank one another like a pair of tennis doubles, but St Michael is as sad and disturbed as his lady friend St Margaret is bonny. The body of the church is gone now, demolished after it became prey to vandalism and even Satanism. Only the fifteenth century tower remains. Once it shone a light to shipping in the Thames. Now it mounts a mobile phone mast, handy for calling help if the dog and I should happen to flounder on a reef.

We passed through one of the prettier spots on this section of Thameside – the Tesco superstore car-park, sited below a six-lane underpass but planted with so many flowering shrubs that you'd swear it was the overflow of a garden centre, which it is. Then in no time we were out on the marsh again. And for the first and only time on the Estuary trail, we became lost.

How do you become lost when you are following a river, indeed, *the* river? The answer had a lot to do with tall hedges and lost signs, and something to do with the drainage ditches that kept blocking the way. You can't just snap your fingers at a drainage ditch. It is full of rampant toads and has a nasty way of drowning you, once the toads have done their worst.

It took us several hours to cross the two miles of marshland between Vange and Fobbing. The endless trial and error was all the more frustrating since we had a constant view of our target – Fobbing Church, another seafarer's beacon, prominent on the high ground. The more our journey was frustrated, the more alluring it seemed. At last we hauled ourselves out of the marshes, scrambled over the last ditch and trespassed our way into the lane at Fobbing. Then we looked back at the hateful bog (a bog is a marsh that you have come to dislike). It lay there, sultry, green and inviting. Not so long ago, before the era of drainage engineers, the marsh was a deadly place, a sucking-pit that could swallow a man in seconds. It is less easy to perish there these days. You would have to be a remarkably overweight man in an unusually rogue puddle. Nevertheless, this marsh was lethal in its own way. It had fractured the trail. Until now, the Estuary Trail had been proceeding in swinging style. Now it had entered hostile territory. Until the footpath disputes could be resolved, it remained a forbidden marsh.

And then, right at the marsh's end, my spirits were lifted in a most unexpected way. Alongside a stretch of (legal, un-mined, undisputed) footpath, someone had planted a garden. For some thirty yards or so, the wild country path passes through a herbaceous border, planted with formal garden blooms.

The wild plants of the marshes, gorse, thistles and yuggas (the King family name for any wild flower we don't know the botanical name for) makes way for valerian, papaver, echinops, and garden cultivars of the delectable yugga plant. This extraordinary garden in the middle of nowhere was lovingly tended, free of weeds, slug-proofed, and, unlike Essex Dog and me, devoid of mildew.

A garden border in itself is no big deal, but a garden without a residence attached, planted purely "to give pleasure to walk-ers who walk through it", is a decidedly big deal. I was ponder-ing the mystery of it all when I bumped into the answer. She is Sonja Stubbs, who lives in Fobbing High Road and has created and tended this footpath garden over many years. The phrase "to give pleasure to walkers who walk through it" is hers.

I had never before encountered such a thing as a footpath garden, made and tended by a member of the public without so much as a community service order placed on them by way of incentive or motivation. Certainly her aim to provide pleasure to ramblers worked on this particular occasion. She raised my spirits right out of the marshland doldrums.

Ahead lay Tilbury. And at Tilbury, the clouds lifted even further. For Tilbury, unlikely as it may seem, is a place of dreams and dreamers – and we were to be caught up in these deter-mined reveries.

Charles Dickens in his study at Gad's Hill in Kent, overlooking the Estuary

A grainy image of the Broomway, the ancient track that runs across the Maplin Sands, parallel to the Foulness shore. It is tested by members of the Essex Field Club in 1907. One of the witches' brooms that marked the route can be seen in the right foreground. It probably came in useful to sweep up after the horses. The Broomway allowed local farmers a level run to market, avoiding the numerous steep-sided creeks that cut into Foulness Island

Cooling Castle in Kent – the only conspicuous bit

They built a monster pub, but nobody came – the British Pilot, at Allhallows

Seven

The Tilbury Dreamers

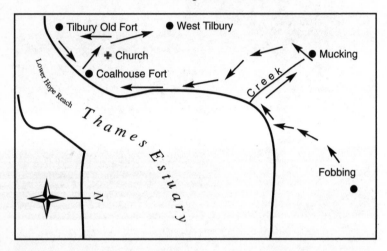

SCENICALLY SPEAKING, the Estuary country between Mucking and Tilbury is a mixture of the grim and the beautiful. In human terms, it has proved far more uncompromising, a place where hard times and tough living went with the turf, not to mention the mud and the black, cold water. Despite, or perhaps in defiance of, such a poverty, this hard terrain has also given rise to a surprising number of visionaries, dreamers of golden dreams. If the dreams that rose on this river-bank have faded, they have left a legacy both in buildings and also in living people, men and women who continue the tradition and dream on.

Leaving Fobbing, I headed back for the river through a countryside that was shabby and under-developed. I warmed to it immediately. The hedges are full of elms that died in the 1970s and still haven't been cleared away. The bijou cottages are boarded up, or still occupied by farming families, people who still know the difference between an old privy and an old biddy, and the dangers of confusing the two. In the farmyards, ancient barns are still tumbling down, their timbers engulfed in ivy and brambles. Such is the desirability of old barns in most parts of the countryside, that in some places, including north Essex, there have been cases of "barn-napping". Barns have disappeared overnight from sites they have occupied for centuries, leaving behind some mightily narked rats in the rain. Yet on low Thameside, the property game somehow operates by a different set of economic rules. The area is so deeply unfashionable that even gipsies seem to avoid it, let alone yuppies. When so much of the countryside has been pruned, manicured, made-over, Ideal Homed and above all, tidied; when even corrugated-iron air-raid shelters are being spruced up and turned into pads for City slickers, this dishevelled stretch of Estuary countryside is positively refreshing. But like other forgotten corners of the Estuary, it can't last.

In an area so close to London, the property pioneers and their reconnaissance parties are bound to arrive soon. More than that, there is already a mighty force for prettification abroad in this part of the country. It takes the unlikely form of Cory Environmental, the rubbish tip folk, whose grassed-over rubbish tips are the silkiest items in this rough landscape. There are few sorts of country sleeker than a landscaped ex-rubbish dump. As London rubbish continues to fill up all available holes, there will be more and more and more of this brave new parkland. Ultimately, city-dwellers are bound to follow their rubbish out of town, and, in course of time, set up home on top of it.

We finally rejoined the river shore just east of Mucking Creek. We looked back at the long line of the refineries. Such a tiny detail – just four miles of industrial plant, £500 million of chemical engineering and a few supertanker moorings – yet they had the effrontery to claim the river as their own. They had cost us dear in terms of the Estuary Trail, taking us away from the waterside and throwing us into the clutches of obdurate farmers and dodgy marshes. Still, the detour made us appreciate the river even more, now that we were back on its banks. Once again, the stirrings of what appeared like true love rumbled somewhere behind the second toggle down on my anorak. "This is God's country, this is my land of milk and honey – and Fairy Snow liquid," I thought, as I watched an empty detergent bottle bobbing downriver on the current. There and then we made a resolution not to leave the river's edge again, just as we came to Mucking Creek and promptly had to break the oath.

The creek took us inland for half a mile, depositing us in the delectably named village of Mucking. It was, of course, a foul place, smeared with filth and litter. Well, actually, and disappointingly, it is quite the opposite. It is just like that other Essex village with a grotpatch name, Ugley, or the celebrated Pratt's Bottom in Kent. Mucking is in reality a delightful, if tiny, village, with a green, spreading chestnut trees, an attractive church (now a private residence) and a cluster of ancient cottages. You could decorate a dozen chocolate boxes with pictures of Mucking and nobody would recognise that the photographs were taken in the same village, let alone that it had a name like a police no-go area. (Do the rubbish tips that abound in this part of the world have names like Lark Sweeting?)

The only other human being around was a man in a van, parked by the green. He had the vehicle's windows closed and was eating a sandwich. As he ate, he nodded to the sound of some inaudible music from the radio. I sidled up to the van and tapped on the window, waving a press card. Looking not altogether happy to see me, he stopped eating, stopped nodding, and wound the glass down.

"King, *Evening Echo*," I said. "I'm just doing a survey. We've got a campaign just started to change the name Mucking to something nicer. The name doesn't do it justice, lowers the tone of the neighbourhood, that sort of thing. I wonder if I could ask your opinion on it."

"I read that paper and I haven't heard of any campaign like that," he said.

"We've just started it," I explained, forbearing to add the words: "five seconds ago."

"I think you should leave these things alone," he said. "I come here to eat my breakfast 'cos it's nice and peaceful, and nobody ever comes here. I think one reason they don't come is 'cos they think with a name like that, it's got to be a shitheap. No, don't muck it about." Which, all things considered, was probably the last word on the subject of Mucking.

We rejoined the river on Lower Hope Reach, a stretch of the Estuary I had walked and written about on a previous occasion. As guidance, I consulted the article from seven years ago. "If you have never walked in this area before, you will be in for a couple of surprises," the younger and more impressionable scribbler had written. "The first is the sheer extent that loneliness can reach. The second is the sheer size of the Thames Estuary. This wild isolation and vastness can be disturbing, but it is also compelling." Laid it on a bit thick didn't he, this guy?

The wildness and isolation hadn't changed, though I was more accustomed to them after walking through Foulness. At this stage, I was more interested in capturing a remarkable optical delusion, which I had also described at the time. It concerned the vanishing of Coalhouse Fort.

More than perhaps anywhere else on the Estuary, this is a land of mud, water, and a sky that blends with the two so that you can hardly see the joins. Dame Nature has taken on a tax office mood. The only vertical features consist of the occasional sign, warning walkers not to step into the quicksand, for reasons that escape me. The colour theme is gunmetal; appropriately, since the Estuary in these parts bristles with aggression. Suddenly, from nowhere, a dirty great fortress emerges on the path ahead of you. You know instantly that it carries enough firepower to blow away an aircraft carrier. You get the uneasy feeling that, on a dull day and in the absence of hostile war-

ships, any rambler not actually sporting the red ensign on his
stern will do for target practice.

Step back a foot or two and the fortress vaporises, becoming
just another vague clump of bushes growing out of a dull patch
of mud, possibly with a civil servant from Agriculture and
Fisheries hidden behind it and counting the number of leaves.
The fort has a dull name to match its dim profile: Coalhouse
Fort. Coalhouse Fort is not dull at all. It is a fascinating display
of the art of camouflage, and I must have spent a good ten minutes, stepping backwards and forwards to watch the fort appear
and disappear, all to Essex Dog's intense irritation and the puzzled curiosity of some Filipino matelots on a passing container-
ship.

The man responsible for Coalhouse Fort was not just your
ordinary camouflage genius. He was no less a body than
General Gordon of Khartoum. This giant among British war-
heroes had been portrayed on the big screen, I recalled, by John
Wayne, or it might have been Arnold Schwarzenegger, or possibly Sigourney Weaver in one of her more macho roles – certainly it needed a tough guy with massive presence to do justice
to this giant among generals.

Gordon is best-known for the tumultuous circumstances of
his murder on the banks of the Nile, at Khartoum, but he had
a life as well as a death, and a significant part of it was spent
here, on the banks of our own answer to the Blue Nile, the
Greyish Brown Thames. I had already boned up on General
Gordon, because today – although I had kept this bad news for
as long as possible from Essex Dog – we were on a history crawl.

Some days before, I had been contacted on the phone by
members of the Tilbury Riverside Action Group. Since one of
the remits of this group is to tidy up the shoreline, and an effec-
tive way of doing this would be to sweep me and my mutt into
the river, I was briefly apprehensive. But they turned out to be
fellow trailblazers. We spoke the same language and walked the
same walk. "We've been reading about your Estuary Walk in

the newspaper, and we'd like you to join us for an organised ramble when you hit Tilbury," said Peter Hewitt, the group's chairman. "Tilbury is a lovely place, There's a lot of history here, so perhaps you could help us sell it."

History? Tilbury? I tried to think of anything in Tilbury that might fit the bill. I knew a midwife from Trinidad who had delivered 9,500 Tilbury babies and could still party all night at the age of 65. She was local history alright, but you could hardly stick a turnstile in front of her and charge tourists £2.50 to view her. Then I looked at the map, and began to realise just how much history of the theme-park variety Tilbury had going begging.

Even so, it's not the sort of place that outsiders tend to think of as historic. It's not, frankly, the sort of place that outsiders think of at all without a bit of a shudder. Anybody who knows Tilbury at all recognises that it is a fine, warm, cheery town, albeit, through no fault of its own, with a battered economic history. Yet its reputation is on a par with the West Bronx. June Brown, one of the Tilbury Action Group's stalwarts, quotes a lad from one of the local youth clubs: "I don't know why Tilbury has got this reputation. I just know I didn't do it."

The Tilbury Action Group members viewed history as one of the keys to the town's regeneration. The immediate dream was the creation of a Tilbury history trail. So here we were, the dog and I, shuffling to and fro in front of Coalhouse Fort, muttering "Now you see it, now you don't", and thinking about the great Victorian general whose spirit still presided here, and who was worth real box office to the town of Tilbury. That's it, it was Charlton Heston who played the role.

Gordon arrived at Tilbury in 1866 to supervise the rebuilding of the fort. A horrible fact had become apparent: ironclad ships could sail up the Thames and bombard London with impunity, and nobody, not even the stalwart company of Beefeaters at the Tower of London, could do a thing to stop it happening. So Gordon, always a man to call when it came to a miracle or two by Tuesday, was deputed to rebuild the old defensive position at Coalhouse in a modern manner. He applied his own unique style to the project. He would race up and down the river in an open boat, rowed by some grunting, sweating Royal Engineers who had pulled the short straw that day. Slow stonemasons would suddenly hear Gordon's voice ring out across the water through a megaphone: "Five minutes gone, boys. We shall never have them back again." That voice was to echo in my mind for much of the rest of the trail, whenever Essex Dog and I slackened our pace for a moment. It's perhaps surprising that Gordon wasn't murdered earlier in his career.

The trouble with Coalhouse Fort, from the tourist point of view, is that it never fired a shot in anger, not even when the Dagenham Girl Bagpipers sailed past on a jaunt. Explosions sell. Stick a picture of an exploding wok on the front cover of a Chinese cookery book and sales multiply. But there are no explosions associated with Coalhouse Fort. It did its job too well. No enemy vessels wanted to venture past a devilish bulk like that, especially one that played peek-a-boo, and then they invented aeroplanes and no longer needed to worry about anything so passé as a land-fort. The killing-grounds around the fort have now been transformed into a pleasant park, and the industrial railway line that transported munitions from the river to the fort is now a bridleway. In other words, the whole place is too peaceable for its own good. However, just a few yards along the approach lane, I knew of a building that would satisfy any tourist's lust for blood and mayhem. It was the local church.

After his visit to the church of St Catharine, the architectural historian Sir Nikolaus Pevsner reported, in a rather perplexed way, that there had obviously been a thirteenth century tower on the church, because the base was still there. But at some time the business end of the tower had gone missing. In fact, there has never been a shred of mystery as to the fate of this tower. It was blown to pieces by cannon fire. By the Dutch. In 1667, they were our Foe of the Month. The sailed up the river, unopposed, boarding where they chose, and for some reason they chose St Catharine's tower. Nobody could quite work out what the tower had done to irk the Dutchmen's ire. The chronicler Morant was of the opinion that, coming from a flat land where everything was neatly level, the sheer height of the tower offended them. Another theory has it that "various inhabitants didst lewdly caper on top of the tower in defiance of all Hollanders" and received a broadside for their cheek. Whatever the explanation, we weren't concerned with the whys and wherefores of history so much as how it could be sold, and an exploding church tower is a unique asset for any place ambitious to sell into the mass-tourist market. I don't know of any other church tower in England that was deliberately blown up, and certainly not in such a way, by a big sailing ship, so far inland, manned by pirates who climbed the rigging in wooden shoes.

If Tilbury was really serious about exploiting its history, then it shouldn't be too difficult to recreate the detonating church-tower, anything up to six times a day for tourists. The great Southend fairground engineer Rob Roberts, who had created one of Europe's most spectacular ghost trains with his bare hands, should be able to rig up a collapsible polyester rig to represent the tower, and I knew any number of resting actors for whom the part of lewdly cavorting natives wouldn't even require any acting. Tilbury really was sitting on more assets than it realised.

What's more, we hadn't even arrived at the jewel in the historic crown. Leaving East Tilbury, we made our way inland, via a series of field-paths and narrow lanes to the companion village of West Tilbury, two miles inland. The view from the top of Gun Hill alone is worth the scramble. But something far more potent awaited us. Just to the north of the village stretches an enormous field. We followed a footpath sign through a hedge and onto the field. It was flat and featureless. Piles of roots stacked up on the headland provided the only visual thrill. Yet this is one of the great historic sites of England. It was here that the great Armada speech was delivered.

In 1588, this wasn't just a muddy field like it is now. It was a much muddier field, thanks to the presence of 23,000 soldiers encamped there, along with their horses and artillery. The Spanish Armada had been sighted in the Channel, England was under imminent threat of invasion and pillage. Within days, the Spanish ships could be making their way up the Thames. Tilbury, protected by a great boom stretched across the ferry passage, was to be the focus of resistance. From their vantage point on Gun Hill, 23,000 pairs of eyes looked anxiously down-river. Just for once, the Estuary was the centre of everybody's attention.

The vast majority of the men assembled on that hill were just civilians, City apprentices and farm lads, who had simply been handed a pike and told to get ready for battle. Many had brought their wives or mums along with them. Unlike the wives and mums, the soldiers were rank amateurs. They were half-starved, poorly armed and had little idea as to what they were supposed to be doing. What could be done to raise the spirit of this ragtag army? Nowadays, they would probably be treated to a show, featuring the rock star flavour of the month and 98-year-old Bob Hope. A show is what this Elizabethan army got. It featured the Lady herself.

Down the river, in a gilded barge, serenaded by forty water-borne musicians, rowed by forty velvet-clad oarsmen, glided Queen Elizabeth I. She was already recognised the world over as Gloriana, 'the Glorious one', and anybody could see why the got the nickname, rather than, for instance, 'Ginger.' From the landing-stage, she transferred into a golden coach and rode up the hill to meet the army, 1,000 horsemen in front of her coach, 1,000 horsemen behind her. For a place that was normally lucky to see one milk-cart a day, it must all have been a bit of a shock.

It was not planned that she should do anything other than exude graciousness and go home. But, seizing the moment, she climbed onto a white horse and delivered, quite off the cuff, one of the most famous speeches in history:

Let tyrants fear ... I know I have the body of a weak and feeble woman, but I have the stomach of a king, and of a king of England too, and think foul scorn that Parma or Spain or any prince of Europe, shall dare to invade the borders of my realm. To which, rather than any dishonour shall grow by me, I myself will be your general, judge and rewarder.

There wasn't a dry eye in the army. Bess had worked her old magic, and another 23,000 males had fallen in love with her. They were all ready to do battle now, although in the event they didn't have to do anything at all, except repeat, far and wide, the words they had heard in this field above the Thames Estuary. Weather and English seamen put paid to the Spanish ships, the army never so much as poked a pike in anger, so the Great Armada speech was, strictly speaking, wasted. Yet Elizabeth's words, like Shakespeare's, have outlived more transient things, like empires, nations, and languages.

Nowhere in West Tilbury is there a memorial to the event, let alone a theme park with a roller-coaster called the Great Armada Terror Ride. Other countries, which shall be nameless, would not have missed such an opportunity, would you, Florida? I told the landlord of the King's Head pub in West Tilbury that he, too, had missed an opportunity. He ought to sell Bess bitter and packets of Francis Drake scratchings. But he told me that very few people came to visit the site, and, by the way, what site was this we were talking about?

There may be no permanent memorial in West Tilbury. But in 1988, the fourth centenary of the great speech, the council rose to the occasion. A giant pageant was organised, with jousting, ox-roasting and, best of all, the great Armada speech re-enacted by the actress Kate O'Mara. And now, four hundred years on, there was an extra reason to anticipate the workings of female magic. Certain tabloids now found the platform to float a vulgar story. It was hinted, in a low-key, 48-point headline sort of way (and without the revealing of sources), that Kate O'Mara/Queen Elizabeth might well unveil for the occasion at Thurrock. When she came to the line: "I know I have the body of a weak and feeble woman," she would prove that she spoke nothing but the truth. A brisk rustle of a mock Tudor halter, and Kate would go down in history as Queen of the world's first topless pageant.

There was an unexpectedly huge turnout on the day. Queen Elizabeth arrived at Tilbury Pier in an ornate barge, accompanied by courtiers and some seasick ladies in waiting. She climbed, with considerable care, onto the white horse that had been groomed, and, it was rumoured, gelded, for the occasion. Then she set off along Fort Road, the country lane that still leads from the jetty to the site of the great speech. Behind her stretched a long line of Yeomen of the Guard, Tudor minstrels, knights in armour, jugglers, Tilbury civic dignitaries, the official Town Crier of London, actors dressed as Tudor rat-catchers and blowsy tarts, vendors of hot dogs (with their frankfurters specially dressed up for the day in little Tudor ruffs), modern media and the general public. Many of the latter looked like the sort of people who wouldn't normally take a great interest in Tudor England, so the story headed: "Could Bess reveal all?" had clearly worked.

The ragtag army eventually reached the field selected for the re-enactment, which was about half a mile south of the actual site, but saved the horse from having to climb Tilbury Hill. "Oyez, oyez, oyez, lend ear to Her Gracious Majesty Queen Elizabeth of England," called the Town Crier. A crowd of around 4,000 needed no further encouragement to gather round, as Kate O'Mara and steed rode forth. Silence fell.

Then, once more, the great words rang out, as they had 400 years beforehand, almost to the minute: "Let tyrants fear. I have always so behaved myself that, under God, I have placed my chiefest strength and safeguard in the loyal hearts and goodwill of my subjects … being resolved, in the midst and heat of battle, to live or die amongst you all, and to lay down, for my God and for my kingdom and for my people, my honour and my blood, even in the dust." Kate O'Mara paused for a moment. The media stood, cameras poised, almost swooning with anticipation.

"I know I have the body …" Ms O'Mara continued. There was a deep intake of breath from the crowd. Kate O'Mara's hand moved to her neck. And at that moment, her horse coughed, snorted, and moved sideways. The horse's action enhanced the drama of the speech. But the animal had upstaged the Queen. She glared at the beast for a moment. Then, resolutely fully clad, she continued: "… of a weak and feeble woman, but I have the heart and stomach of a king, and of a king of England too." A heart-breaking sigh came from the assembled rank of photographers, as it became clear that, whatever her original intentions, Ms O'Mara's robes were going to remain firmly draped.

Afterwards, the Town Crier said to me: "She certainly got a good response from the crowd. Did you hear them during the bit about 'the body of a weak and feeble woman'. That speech still has the power to move people after 400 years, doesn't it."

The Armada Pageant provided a great shot in the arm for Tilbury at the time, but you can only have one of those every 88th year of the century. Everyday reality had settled back for a long time when I arrived at Tilbury Old Fort to meet the members of the Tilbury Action Group.

They were going to introduce me and anybody else who turned up this Sunday morning to the pleasures of the Two Fort Walk. Much of this stretch had been trailblazed by the Action Group. They had restored an old right of way through a rubbish dump, thereby creating a significant link in the Estuary Trail. For Essex Dog and me, it involved backtracking for two miles along the riverside path. In the present company, I would have walked all the way back to Foulness.

They were clustered around the portico of the old fort, and as soon as I set eyes on them, I knew that we were soul-mates. We shared a mistress. Others might see Madame Estuary as a dowdy old crone, but we knew the silky charms that lay beneath. Provided that we didn't end up brawling over possession of her, we were going to get along just fine.

It was at this stage that I got to meet Pete Hewitt, the chairman of the group. Pete is a retired policeman who has spent his working life on the Tilbury patch. He would arrange for his beats to cover areas of the town that he wanted to study. There's nothing like a slow two-mph plod when it comes to really getting to know somewhere. "I just love this place, every square inch of it is history," he told me.

As we retraced our steps along the shore, Pete was able to point out features that we had missed first time round – like Coal Beach. This is a stretch of foreshore, close to the power station, that is coloured black rather than the more conventional sandy colour favoured in fashionable seaside resorts. Yet locals still enjoy picnicking there, maybe because it is about the one place where it is possible to enjoy a beach barbecue simply by setting fire to the beach.

I wouldn't have known this without Pete as guide, nor would I have known about the Jubilee Marsh. The marsh looks just like any other stretch of rough grazing land; it is in fact a put-up job. Purist naturalists would consider it a con-marsh. If so, it has certainly conned a large number of marshland flowers, who have happily settled here and have the seeds to prove it.

The truth begins immediately beneath the roots of these plants, where anybody who cares to stick their finger into the ground will discover spoil from London's Jubilee Underground line, laid on top of an exhausted rubbish tip. Travellers on the Jubilee trains may feel that they have got the best of the bargain, what with all that unwanted soil dumped in Essex, while they enjoy themselves stranded in the darkness during a signal failure. In fact, Tilbury is undoubtedly the winner. It has gained a new marsh and a new chapter to its history. "The hardiness of a place like this is part of the character of the place," says Peter Hewitt. "We don't want to take away from it, just make it more accessible."

As we neared the end of the walk, Peter Hewitt asked: "So, do you think that we've got much to offer?"

I breathlessly listed the various historic attractions that the dog had whined at earlier that morning. "Going by the whine count, I'd say that you were really well off," I said. Peter agreed, but then he said: "Do you know what I think the real attraction is?"

"I'd say the Queen Elizabeth site. Now, if you had a statue of Queen Elizabeth ... don't sculpt too many clothes and you might even get the *News of the World* interested ... If you do it in Roman style with a toppling toga you can get away with a bit of nudity ... Okay, I know she was Tudor, not Roman, but ..."

"I'd say we're walking on the main attraction," interrupted Peter, quietly.

"What do you mean?"

"The path," said June Brown. "If we persuade the hikers to come and walk along the river, that could be the key to regenerating Tilbury."

"It's the river that's going to do it," said Peter. "I've known this stretch of river all my life, and I know that it's magic."

I looked around at the walkers of the Action Group. Here were more semi-official enthusiasts, achieving small miracles on little except a diet of dreams and fresh air. We shared an affliction. They too had been bitten by the Estuary bug. The symptoms were beginning to become recognisable – a certain special lollop as they sprung along the riverside path; and a fervent glint in the eye, the result of staring at far-off places on the other side of the Estuary. Any final doubts on this matter disappeared after what came next. It was the ultimate wild visionary Estuary inspiration.

"Of course, they'll need some sort of special attraction."

"They've got all the history they can want," I said. "There's a fort at each end. What more do they want. Loyalty cards?" I noticed one of the enthusiasts scribble down this idea.

"We're blessed with history, but we were thinking of something more modern. How about a bridge?"

"There is a bridge. A six-lane job. Just up the river. I'm sure I saw one there."

"Not another great road bridge like the Thurrock one. A pedestrian bridge."

I looked across to the Kent shore, over that great stretch of water, and the river seemed to mutter "stuff this diet" and expand in girth even as I looked at it. "It would be incredibly expensive," I said. "And it would have to clear the ships' funnels. It would have to really, like, soar. How much do you think it would cost?"

"I don't know. £20 million. £25 million. It would be the most expensive pedestrian bridge in the world, probably. But people would come to see it from miles around. It would really bring people into the area."

"Do you think it will ever happen?"

"Nothing's impossible. Look at what we've achieved so far. Look at this path."

The path didn't look so spectacular, just a patch of cleared ground wending its way through the scrub of the rubbish-heap. But I knew the battles, the tenacity, the bureaucracy and often the sheer hard cash needed to lay down one of these narrow ramblers' highways. After this, a £25 million bridge might just be a doddle.

The more you considered it, the more appealing the bridge seemed. It wasn't just a majestic vision, it was a sensible idea, provided they remembered to put in railings and didn't invest millions inserting a built-in wobble. That was what the Estuary needed to tie it together – a triumphal entry arch, built by dreamers, to cater for adventurers. All those on the Kent shore who spent their lives staring across at Essex could finally walk across to confirm their worst prejudices. And vice versa. But it wouldn't be a humble journey. Such a bridge would transfer a humble walk into an eagle's soar.

There was still a mile or so to go, and Peter continued to point out the features on the way – the World War II radar tower, the house that had once belonged to a former gunfighter from the Wild West. But I think I must have gone unusually quiet.

The churchyard of St Catharine had been transformed since the dog and I had first visited it that morning. There were flowers and bunting, and a huge walker's tea of sandwiches, homemade cakes, and scones had been laid out. It looked like a wake for a Women's Institute president. "It's a walkers' brunch," Pete Hewitt explained. "I think we deserve it." But we'd only walked two miles. Lucky these people don't operate at the end of the Pennine Way, really.

We had done walking for the day, except for one more short stroll round the churchyard. After a minute or two, I located the grave of Hamilton Williams, the retired gunfighter. He was another man clearly bitten by Estuary fever.

This was a man who had hunted bison on the prairies; witnessed battles with Sioux "injuns"; watched as a great paddlesteamer sank into the waters of the Mississippi; ridden and fought with the Mounted Rangers in the American Civil War; been rescued from the gallows within seconds of hanging; run a gambling salon; and been a wagon-master, escorting prairie schooners through hostile country to the edge of the frontier. Hamilton Williams made a fortune in the New World, and could have lived out his twilight years in comfortable billets anywhere in the world. The place he chose was Tilbury, by the Estuary. "Nobody can quite understand why he came here, when he had so many places to choose from," said Peter Hewitt. But I knew, and so did he, really.

With my back to Hamilton's gravestone, I began to fiddle and doodle with my plate of sandwiches. My mum always told me not to play with my food, and of course she was right. Food is for eating, especially Tilbury teas. But on this occasion, I was doing something constructive with the sandwiches. I was building a model. It was a prototype. A bridge. For the moment, it was only a bridge made of bread.

But one day ...

The grave of one-time Wild West gunfighter Hamilton Williams, in East Tilbury

Eight

Gravesend Discovered

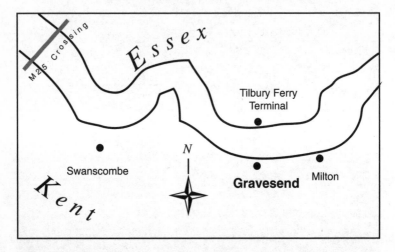

FOR THE first time, we felt seasick. This was quite an achieve-ment, since we were by now some eighteen miles inland. Still, the heaving, bilious green river had all the meanness of a rough ocean. So did the sea-life. A discarded fish n' chip wrapper swept past, Tilbury's answer to the flying-fish of the southern oceans.

One day, hopefully, the dog and I would be able to soar over this stretch of water on the Dreamers' bridge, even if we were both confined to wheelchairs by then. Meanwhile, we had to settle for whatever form of crossing was available. We were waiting to board the Tilbury-Gravesend ferry, or what was left of it. Not so long ago, this was the busiest short-haul ferry serv-ice in western Europe. Almost all traffic from east of the Great North Road passed over these dirty, choppy waters, whether it was headed for the Channel Ports or just a naughty weekend with a promising pen-pal in Brighton. Tilbury town developed its own smoggy micro-climate as a result of all the car fumes, and many of the buildings on the ferry approach are still black-ened with the fumes. Now the ferry had dwindled to 200 pas-sengers a day, although today it was due to be 201, boosted by one man and a miserable green waif on four legs who had always hated boats.

The pontoon at Tilbury is built to rise and fall with the tide. It is an impressive piece of engineering: it can take and has taken ocean-going liners, but nowadays mostly has to content itself with charging mooring fees to the occasional exhausted surfboarder. This desolate spot was the turning point of the walk.

True, for most people, the head of the Estuary is probably symbolised by the soaring Queen Elizabeth Bridge at Thurrock, four miles upriver, where the mighty force of motion, the Thames, meets that mighty force of slow-motion, the M25 motorway. Six lanes of traffic cross here, but there are also two further, very narrow, lanes, designed for pedestrians. Over years of crossing the bridge by car, I had never set eyes on a single human using this track. Presumably even would-be suicides find the vertigo too much to take. But, hey, we were forging an Estuary trail here, and this is the age of pedestrianism. So I rang the bridge authorities to ask permission to write an article. A quaking photographer would join me, trying hard not to let handshake affect the quality of her pictures, and the piece would be headed: *It's just a big footbridge really*. But there was no deal.

"We have a blanket policy," I was told. "No public and no media on the walkway. There are no exceptions."

"Yes, but you can make an exception for us, can't you," I wheedled.

"We're very sorry, but it's too dangerous. You could get blown off the bridge even in relatively low wind conditions."

"So, I'll wear a bungee rope. Think of the publicity if I fall off and keep bouncing up and down. It will really put your lit-tle bridge on the map."

The press officer politely told us that, with around 40,000 vehicles a day passing over it, the bridge had all the attention that it craved already, thank you. That was the end of the matter, although I did discuss with the photographer the possibility of an illicit crossing at dead of night, roped together. But who do you call if you find yourself dangling from the Thurrock road bridge at 2am? The AA? We copped out.

Besides, Tilbury Docks lay in our path. Tilbury Docks are a fascinating network of manmade lagoons and human-interest stories. From the walker's point of view, though, they are Thames-side bogie No 1. They block off access to the river for much of the last stretch to the Thurrock Bridge.

In any case, Tilbury-Gravesend, the historic crossing-point of the upper Estuary, has a fair claim to the title Head of the Estuary. It has operated the main Kent to Essex ferry crossing since before the two counties even answered to their names. And at Gravesend, the Thames pilots have made their base for over 100 years. This, then, was to be the Estuary turning-point.

I had to admit to a certain amount of trepidation. Something deep inside me said that this particular patch of Estuary was more dangerous than being blown off the Thurrock Road Bridge, let alone merely crossing it.

When I was a child, we had a neighbour named Captain Hutchinson. In his last years before retirement, he operated as an Estuary pilot. Captain Hutchinson had sailed the oceans in wooden square-riggers and been torpedoed in mid-Atlantic. "But I'm telling you, young fella," he said, "there's no more terrifying stretch of water in the world than that Tilbury reach. We lost eight fellows just the other day. Small boat turns over, water fills their sea-boots. Glug, swish, thump, straight to the bottom. And then, just when you think the worst is over, the tide gets them. That sort of thing happens so often they don't even bother to report it in the papers." Knowing what I now knew about local papers, they were probably just short-staffed, but this didn't stop Captain Hutchinson's long-ago words from echoing in my ears as I surveyed Tilbury reach.

There was also the matter of what lay on the far side. Gravesend! The town sat there in grim mystery, a cluster of wharves, sheds and odd-looking silos, perhaps containing reserve supplies of khaki dye and pea-soup for the river. Other faraway places whisper: "Come to me, come to me." This one said: "You want to start something? No? Well bog off then."

The odds are stacked up against Gravesend. For a start, there is its very name. While I waited for the ferry, I planned a few twinning ceremonies for the town. *Gravesend, Kent, England, partnered with Tombstone, Arizona; Woewoe, China, and Dead, Hungary*, the signs would read on entry to the town. The towns of the Thames Estuary are noted for their grim, though honest names – Mucking, Pit-on-sea, Grays, Vange (what's a vange? Ask whatever cat brought it into the house. It's basically something edible but that you definitely do not want to eat). But for truly uninviting names, Gravesend takes the vange.

As if all this wasn't enough, my own dear Kentish-born wife had added her own forceful opinion. "*Walk* through Gravesend," she gasped. "You can't do it. It's much too rough! Especially around the Milton area! You'll be mugged."

"You can get mugged anywhere these days. Anyway, I've got the dog."

"She won't be much use against a mugger. She won't even bite the Tooth Fairy."

"No, but they'll take one look at her and realise any owner of a dog like that is not worth trying to rob. Besides, as you know, whenever anybody tries to mug me, I always end up interviewing them for the paper."

My wife shook her head. "You just don't know what it's like on the other side of the water." Then she lowered her voice to a whisper, checked the room for bugs, and whispered: "Couldn't you just, say, for instance, take the bus along the route like any normal person would do."

"I can't do that!" I said, indignantly. "I'm blazing a hiking trail. Other walkers are going to be following after me. They're going to trust me and any route I give them."

"So you're quite happy to lead all those other walkers into the lions' den. You're going to hand over all those trusting ramblers to the Milton muggers, while you amble through safely because you're too scruffy to be worth the effort."

"Er ... Well, yes, something like that."

In the end, we compromised. As a warning to other ramblers, I devised a brand new "Walkers: Beware Muggers" symbol. This would be placed on any maps of the route. Ideally, they would also be placed as signs along the trail itself. Somehow, though, I doubted whether Kent County Council would subsidise these. As for my own protection, I agreed to beg any likely-looking mugger for the price of a drink. Not only would this underline that I was not worth robbing. It might actually *get* me a free drink if the mugger was in a generous mood.

None of this was calculated to paint the best possible image of Gravesend, as I squinted queasily across the green waters at the indeterminate collection of buildings on the far side. Yet even more powerful than any sense of menace, there was an aura of strangeness about the place. I was a good Essex Boy about to cross the water. I was set to become the nearest thing that the *Southend and Basildon Evening Echo* ever had to a foreign correspondent. There were towns 8,000 miles away, whose people spoke languages that I couldn't reproduce vocally without sticking a drain-plunger down my throat, and I knew their streets and watering-holes better than I knew this town – a town that I had been staring at all my life. Were there other spots that I thought I knew, but didn't really know at all? I started to examine my toes and knees with new-found interest. What unsuspected secrets did they hold? Nobody who hasn't worked for a provincial newspaper can quite appreciate the sense of visceral angst and almost criminal unease as you cross over the invisible border into another newspaper's territory.

A blob on the water grew bigger, revealed itself as the licensed ferryboat Micawber, and thudded into its perch at the terminal. Just three passengers disembarked, one of them clutching a moped. Two oranges in a net dangled from the handlebar. "Is that a decoration?" I asked. "No," he said. "I just like to snack while I'm riding." The dog and I were the only ones making the voyage back again. We boarded and introduced ourselves to Captain Dennis Jones, the skipper in charge of a crew consisting of himself and ... well, that about wrapped matters crew-wise.

A quiet, but beaming, man, Captain Jones had been on the ferries, man and boy, since 1949. He had started as a cabin-boy in the days when the ferries were ships, still ran on steam-power, and employed a crew of sixteen. Now the ferry runs on diesel and Captain Dennis Jones. He himself was due to retire at the end of the year.

"You picked the wrong time to come and talk," he said, wistfully.

"Why, are you otherwise engaged?" I asked, rather surprised, looking around at the empty boat.

"No, I mean you should have come thirty years ago, before the tunnel and all that got under way."

Upriver, traffic thundered over and beneath the river at the Dartford-Thurrock crossing – Captain Jones's nemesis.

"They were good old days," Captain Jones mused as we chugged out into the river. "On Bank Holidays you'd see the cars queuing for miles back into Essex."

It seemed funny to find somebody nostalgic for vanished traffic. Norman Bates, owner of the Psycho motel, was the only other example I could call to mind.

"I don't suppose the people stuck in the cars thought of them as the good old days."

"No?" asked Captain Dennis Jones in surprise. "Well, if you say so. But I think they were happy enough. They used to bring little buckets with them and clean their cars while they waited.

Still, I don't really know about the people in the cars. All I knew about was the water and they were good times then. The place really boomed. There were men on the dockside, men on the boats, other boats out on the water, men directing the traffic. Then came the new tunnel and then the bridge and suddenly the cars all went away and didn't want us any more. And gradually the other men have all gone and now I'm standing here, taking the ferry across the river on my own. It's a funny thing, you know – when I was a boy deckhand, I used to look up at the skipper on the bridge and think, one day, I'm going to be up there. Well, I achieved my ambition, and I'm standing on that bridge, but I never dreamed that I'd be the only man left there."

Captain Jones now did something I had never heard from a sailor before – he was rude about his own command. I had always understood that it was the worst of maritime bad luck for a skipper to slag off his own ship. "Of course, this isn't what I call a proper ferry," he snorted. I nervously marked the whereabouts of the life-rafts as he proceeded to pour abuse onto the very decks on which he stood.

"Look at this," he said. "It doesn't even have a wheel. It steers with levers. My son said to me, 'you know dad, that's not a real boat, it's a floating fruit machine.'"

Even to my un-nautical eyes, the Micawber didn't look quite normal. She lacked normal boat-shaped features like bows or curves. Every time there was a bow-wave from, say, a drowned cat floating past, she heaved and wallowed as though some brawny nautical nurse was trying to inject local anaesthetic into her beam ends. Still, she seemed to move through the water fast enough, quite unfazed by all the raspberries being blown at her by her captain.

"With the old ferries," sneered Captain Jones, "you'd come alongside, toss a rope and a bloke would make you fast. With this … this … box thing that we're on, it does all that for you. Just plugs itself into a hole in the jetty. My son said to me, 'you know dad, that's not a boat, that's just a floating bung.'"

"It's a quite revolutionary design," I said. I knew for a fact that the White Horse Ferry Company were immensely proud of their design. They had started out as just a property company, with a portfolio of buildings on the waterfront. Looking out of the window of their show-house, the executives had started to take an interest in the river, and, before they knew it, they were heavily into boats and running the ancient Tilbury Ferry route.

"Oh it's cheap to run alright," snorted Captain Jones, as though this was yet another blemish in the little ferry's soul. "My son said to me, 'you know dad, that's not a ferry, that's a cost-cutting exercise.'"

I had boarded the vessel with the hopes of tapping Captain Dennis Jones for some of his memories, but I had to ride all the way to Gravesend, and then back to Tilbury with him, all the time bad-mouthing the Micawber, before I could steer him back to the past.

It wasn't until the third leg across the Thames that things began to stir in Captain Dennis Jones's deep memory, and then at last the stories began to pour out. I gave up all pretence of casual conversation and hauled my battered shorthand pad out of my rucksack. Captain Jones looked at it the way he probably looks at a dead conger eel wrapped round his propeller in mid-stream, but he kept on talking.

He told me about the Indian sultan who had arrived at Tilbury on a P&O liner some time in the 1920s, complete with sulky Western blonde mistress and – the real love of his life – his elephant. The elephant and the mistress, between whom no love was lost, had both been packed onto the car-ferry for the crossing, all set on the far side to catch the London District and Chatham Railway for Dover and thence the south of France, while the Sultan proceeded to London to pay his respects to the King. The elephant and the mistress spent the crossing staring daggers at one another.

There were tales of the wartime years, and fuel shortages. One skipper received, as a Christmas present from his wife, half a ton of driftwood. She had slowly collected it together over the year as a sign of devotion. "It's just what I wanted, darling," he told her.

Captain Jones also recalled the days when many men who worked along the water not only could not swim, but refused to learn. On one ferry crossing, an elderly and particularly crusty deckhand fell into the river.

"Now Captain Bales, who was skipper when this chap took his dive, he was one of the old school," said Captain Jones. "'I told you, you should have bloody well have learnt to swim,' he bellows from the bridge."

"'It's bad luck to learn to swim,' shrieks the drowning bloke, before his head disappears under the water."

I was so busy scribbling down these tales that I almost failed to notice when the little hi-tech ferry thudded into its high-tech docking system and was grabbed by those automatic arms that decidedly did not set Captain Dennis Jones's heart on fire.

Whatever it was that I had expected, it wasn't this. A picture-postcard medieval inn, built on piles that were dug into the water. An elegant black-and-white Victorian pier. A row of sleekly expensive-looking modern flats, stretching along the riverside path.

"Er, is this our stop?" I asked Captain Jones.

"This is it – Gravesend, as usual," announced the gentle Captain Jones, slightly puzzled.

The dog and I stepped ashore and looked around us in surprise. This, then, was the grubby blur of what looked like shantytown when viewed from the Essex shore. But it had transformed into a gracious and attractive town. Once again, the tidal river had worked an act of perverse alchemy.

The old inn is called the Three Daws and it marks the start of the footpath called the Saxon Shore Way. For several miles at least, this path hugs the waterside, all set to do our trail-finding work for us. Just for once, I wouldn't have to think, constantly, about finding our way. I could just follow the signs, and there would be time to scribble whingeing notes about the problems of pioneering and route-finding. We were keen to get on our way – yet, quite unexpectedly, Gravesend waylaid us.

The name is unfair. It doesn't look at all like the sort of place where a corpse says: "Blimey, I'm not hanging around in a dump like this." Captivated by the tall Georgian houses and the waterside parks, I sought out the information centre, studied the local history of Gravesend for ten minutes, wrote "Gravesend: Guide: £10" onto my expenses form, and set out to explore the town.

Gravesend, it turns out, was never a dump. Indeed, it used to be so posh that the Germans raided it with a Zeppelin in 1915. They reckoned that by dropping bombs on Gravesend, it would be possible to wipe out a disproportionate number of the English upper classes in one fell swoop. Long before Southend or Sheerness were built, Gravesend was the capital town of the Estuary. The place has always had everything going for it except, of course, its name. Sailing ships returning from the most ungodly parts of the world would make their first landfall here. The town's boatmen enjoyed the rights of "Long Passage", the entitlement to barge passengers from the big ships upriver to central London. Far from being the end of the world, it was traditionally the beginning.

And this was the town that I and other rude Essex types had been slagging off from across the river all our lives. The effect of discovering the real Gravesend was almost cataclysmic. I was undergoing an eye-opener, a road to Damascus, I was giving up a 40-a-day smoking habit, I was converting to Catholicism, I was giving up Catholicism.

The place, I discovered, had a similarly mad tonic effect on others before me. At the dawn of the Victorian age, the first steamboats on the Thames used to carry Londoners downriver for a day out at – Gravesend. "This town has been long and universally known as the goal of every young cockney's Sunday excursions," it was written at the time. Cockneys didn't get out much, then.

There was even an attempt to turn Gravesend into a seaside resort, dubbed Gravesend-on-Sea. The obvious barrier to such an enterprise – the fact that Gravesend isn't actually on the coast – does not seem to have deterred the developers one bit. After all, the smog over the river meant that the opposite shore was often invisible, just as it is with the real sea.

I had become an avid tourist, systematically ticking off every spot in town with the slightest historical interest. I even offered to give a sleeping wino the price of a bottle of Wincarnis, if he would move away from the Victorian clock-tower and allow me to photograph it unencumbered.

We roamed from the Magnificent Clarendon Hotel, past the remains of the Henry VIII fort. I admired the newly restored Regency columns in the crescent around the clock tower, and used the telephoto lens, paparazzi style, on the statue of the young Queen Victoria. Then we walked past rows of old sea-captains' houses to Windmill Hill, a freak green bump in the middle of town with a sweeping view across the Estuary. We had the place to ourselves, apart from some teenagers eating fish and chips (so we had discovered the source of all those cod-wrappers that flap down the Estuary; even David Livingstone never achieved that!). Indeed, wherever we went, we appeared to be the only sightseers in town.

As a climax to the tour, we then rolled up to Gravesend's most famous tourist attraction, the statue of Princess Pocahontas, native American aristocrat and Walt Disney cartoon heroine. As luck would have it, I had recently watched the video Pocahontas with my children. I knew all about the lady. She could dive unharmed from 200-feet waterfalls, swing from trees and scare the bejesus out of grizzly bears and alligators. Her ability with a bow-and-arrow – she could land an arrow in a man's bottom from a range of 250 yards, and would do so unhesitatingly if he tried any hanky-panky – has made her a heroine to generations of feminists. This wild warrior woman, this queen of the virgin North American forests, somehow ended up in Gravesend.

Every American school-child knows the romantic story of Pocahontas. The leader of the first permanent English colony in America, at Jamestown, Virginia, was one Captain John Smith – well, anyway, that was the name he used to check in for the night at colonial settlements. Captain Smith was alone in the woods when he was captured by resident natives, who tied him up ready for a painful death. But Pocahontas, the daughter of the chieftain Powhaten, threw herself in front of John Smith. "I beseech you dear father," she implored, "not to take the life of one so fair and noble of appearance, but rather to strike my own bosom in his stead." Impressed by this display of devotion, Powhaten relented and decided not to shoot either of them. That, in any case, was the tale as told by Smith and Pocahontas when they emerged, understandably dishevelled, from the woods.

Unfortunately, at this stage the real-life romantic story goes awry, causing immense problems to the Walt Disney scriptwriters. By rights, Pocahontas should have married John Smith and lived happily ever after as Mrs P Smith, housewife. Instead, she married another settler, John Rolfe, whose life she had never saved, not even once. Then she went to live in Gravesend. Even the story spinners of Mickey Mouseland couldn't turn this great anti-climax into a cartoon ending. Disney's Pocahontas ends with John Smith heading home to England and Pocahontas promising to visit him, more in the manner of a spinster auntie than a nubile forest poppet. It is all very anti-climactic, but alas, it was the anticlimax of real life.

We had completed our tour of historic Gravesend, and very enlightening it was too. It's not often that you find a swan masquerading as a dead emu. I made a silent promise never to write another line in a property article, beginning: "Desirable freehold in one of Tilbury's more sought-after streets, shielded from any views of Gravesend." Yet there was also an odd feeling of dissatisfaction, of incompleteness. It was those old newspaper instincts, stirring yet again, for all my attempt to stop the presses.

I knew all about the history and architecture of Gravesend, but what about the here and now? And what about the people? On the Essex shore, I was in touch with almost everything on the patch. I knew the politics, scandals, personalities, organisational and criminal structures of the area, which hot-dog stands would give you food poisoning, and which hospital casualty department not to go to when it happened. These were just the little things you took for granted when you worked a local beat. Yet here, just half a mile across the water, I knew nothing about what was going on. I didn't even know when there had last been a proper murder, or how the victim felt about it. Gravesend was a party to which I had never been invited, and now I wanted to gatecrash it.

Eventually the urge to find out about such things became insuperable. I crept furtively into a newsagent and purchased a copy of the local rag, the *Gravesend Messenger*. Somewhere in here there must be a story that I could stick my nose into. The sense of guilt was strong. I had sworn to give local news a miss. Part of the reason for seeking out the Estuary Trail was to find a straight and narrow path to stick to. Yet here I was, an alien in somebody else's newspaper territory, sniffing at stories that were no concern of mine. It was the ultimate dereliction of professional etiquette. It felt sinful. It felt wicked. It felt great.

Things certainly were happening in Gravesend that week. For a start, war had been declared. Yes: *War declared*, screamed the headline. How exciting! Admittedly it was only on fly-tippers, but anything that held out the prospect of tanks on the streets and spivs being mortared in their pick-ups was bound to appeal to readers. A man had beaten up a woman for spilling his beer. He appeared wholly baffled and bemused at finding himself in court, and was quite unable to understand that he had done anything unreasonable under the circumstances.

A rape victim had seen her attacker put behind bars, a new Sikh temple was nearing completion, and several correspondents were seeking to tidy up the town. "Quite right too, it's in a disgusting state," I snorted, as the wind picked up a page of the *Gravesend Messenger* and whipped it down the street.

And then I saw it. A story so perfect, so tailored to the occasion, so rich in prospects, that I had to shut my eyes and reopen them again after five seconds, just to confirm that this double-page spread in the *Gravesend Messenger* was for real. It was, and like all good hacks under such circumstances, I fell upon my knees and gave thanks, having first checked with my rambler's compass that I was facing west, towards old Fleet Street.

It was a marvellous story, and the wonderful thing was that the *Kent Messenger* team had no idea just how good a tale it was that had unfolded in their midst. Written by *Messenger* reporter Mike Cooper, it was headed: *Sherlock and the case of the Missing Hand.* Its subject matter was a major, indeed grave, Gravesend scandal. Some unspeakable bounder had stolen a piece of Queen Victoria. In the depths of night, he had crept up and removed the right hand from the stone statue of the great queen in Darnley Road. Now her majesty wanted it back. "Do you know what has happened to the missing hand? Can you help Sherlock Holmes solve the crime?" the *Kent Messenger* begged its readers. As it happened, I did, and could.

Clearly, the inhabitants of Gravesend were as unfamiliar with the Essex shoreline as most Essex people were ignorant of Gravesend. If only Gravesenders had taken the trouble, as the dog and I had, to blaze a new trail around the Estuary, they would have known that there was another statue of Queen Victoria, in Southend. And that statue held the answer to their own Victorian mystery.

The Southend-on-Sea statue sits on the cliff-tops, facing out toward the pier. It depicts a much older Victoria than the Gravesend statue. The Kent statue shows an eager young slip of a thing, the Southend statue depicts a stout and elderly

Empress of India, with a look under her nose that says: "If you'd had to sit up here all these years on a wet throne you wouldn't be amused either." Yet the two statues represent the same person, and for all the differences in their age, both Queens share something in common. They are staring out towards the Thames Estuary, the great artery of the British Empire that led to the imperial capital, almost as if they appreciate the muddy channel.

In fact, these two queens shared something else apart from identity. For over twenty years, the Southend Victoria was also missing her right hand. This missing member became the main source of her fame. She was recognised all over town as "the one-handed statue" or even just "the Stump." History teaching being what it is in schools these days, quite a lot of Southenders had never heard the name Queen Victoria, or just associated it with an East End pub. But everybody knew the one-handed statue.

Then one night, shortly before I embarked on the Estuary walk, an observant passer-by rang the Southend newsdesk with momentous tidings. Queen Victoria's hand was back. At some time, under mysterious circumstances, a new stone hand had been attached to the stump. Who or what had done it, nobody could say. Under examination, the hand appeared as if it might not be quite so new after all. There was slight green at the wrist. This suggested that the stonework was old enough for lichens to have become established. Local UFO-watchers reckoned that it bore all the hallmarks of little green Martian stonemasons. Whoever was responsible, however, the conclusion was inevitable. The Southend Victoria, desperate to get her bits back together again and regain her dignity, has crossed the Estuary and snaffled a hand from her younger counterpart.

Yet nobody made the connection between the two statues. The reason was simple, of course. In the best tradition of towns on either side of the Estuary, neither town had an inkling as to what was taking place on the opposite shore. The dog and I were typical. We had passed the Southend Queen Victoria most days of our lives. On several occasions, the dog had shown her respect by trying to dig up some of the Council's bedding plants from beneath the statue. Yet until today, we had had no idea that the Queen's younger self had sat facing us down the years, just out of sight on the other side of the river. It followed, as an obvious fact, that nobody on the opposite shore had made a connection, or pondered how the Southend Victoria's hand had reappeared at almost exactly the time that the Gravesend one went AWOL.

Still, there was no cause for complaint. Here was a scoop indeed. It offered a rare link between the two sides of the river. It also provided the perfect excuse to make oneself at home in somebody else's newspaper patch. The headline wrote itself: *Hands across the Estuary.*

We sat ourselves down under the statue of Princess Pocahontas (complete with both her hands; no vandal messes with the anatomy of a native American warrior, even a metal one). I took out my notebook, found something that looked more like a writing implement than a boot-scraper after ten minutes hunting through the outer pockets of my rucksack, and there and then I prepared a story to launch in the *Gravesend Messenger.*

By the time I had finished, the afternoon was well advanced. We had planned to walk through the great, empty stretch of marshland that lies east of Gravesend. But a lethal combination of Captain Jones, Gravesend, and now an unexpected scoop had wrecked that plan. The marshes would have to wait for another day, when we would march resolutely through the town, ignoring its distractions. There remained, however, just enough time in the day for one last walking mission.

We headed, now, not east for the mouth of the Estuary, but west – back towards London, defying the whole purpose of the enterprise. The manoeuvre felt unnatural. My feet dragged, every movement was sluggish and difficult, as in one of those nightmare dreams where you are desperately trying to force your limbs into action in order to run away from a timeshare salesman. But we had a significant goal – nothing less than the most important historical site in England.

We plodded along the pavement by the old London-bound road out of Gravesend. The road hugs the higher ground, 400 yards back from the river. The slight elevation makes a surprising, dramatic difference. Alongside the road are Georgian terraces and old inns. Further downhill there are factories, grotty wharves for loading and unloading the smellier sorts of cargoes, and junkyards. In the near distance looms the vast, soaring bulk of the Queen Elizabeth bridge, looking from here as if it is constructed from used Ford Capri hub-caps, picked up at the junkyards. No tourist visits this haunted, half-beautiful, half-menacing landscape from one season to the next. Yet this is the very heart of history.

Two miles along the road we turned left, into the narrow passageway called Craylands Lane. We passed under the railway bridge, then turned right onto a footpath. It was a villainous place. The path ran between the railway embankment and a long-disused gravel-pit. Dilapidated rolling-stock clanked along the rail track. The south London rail safety record being what it is, we anticipated a train on our heads at any moment. I would not have bothered to coiff or de-flea Essex Dog that morning had I realised. On the other side of the path, the prospect was even less enticing. The pit-edge sloped sharply down into oblivion. It had been colonised by all the hardest, most streetwise plants – elders, blackthorns, ivy and brambles. It oozed dankness. Yet for all the abundance of scrubby trees, no birds sang in the darkness of the pit. A dilapidated sign on the lip of the quarry was just legible. "Danger – Keep Out," it said. Funnily enough, we had already made that decision for ourselves.

In this decayed hole, the story of the human race begins in Britain. This is the home, the Ideal Home, of Swanscombe

Man. The Guinness Book of Records states the facts with succinct authority. "The oldest definite human remains ever found in Britain are pieces of a brain case from a specimen of homosapiens, recovered in June 1935 and March 1936 by Dr Alvan T Marston from the Boyn Hill Terrace in the Barnfield Pit, near Swanscombe, northern Kent." This doesn't quite tell the full story. The good Dr Marston earned his living as a dentist, and took a keen professional interest in anything to do with decayed teeth. It was when he noticed a particularly neglected set of molars, teeth that hadn't seen the active end of a toothbrush for 230,000 years, sticking out of the quarry, that the story of Swanscombe Man begins.

Just when he seemed to have made a break for freedom, Homo Swanscombe's remains were handed over to the London Natural History Museum. They now live in a cardboard-box, somewhere in the depths of Kensington, where they will no doubt gather dust for another 230,000 years. However, an exact replica is on display at the nearest appropriate location, the little town museum in Dartford.

Here the half-skull, technically an occipital, is set against a painted background depicting the sort of environment in which Swanscombe Man lived, and, as the skull testifies, died. A gaggle of hairy nudists are pursuing some deer across a wild marsh landscape, thinly spattered with trees. The sun is shining and the climate is balmy, but apart from that, and the absence of shiny designer underwear, the scene is recognisably Thames Estuary.

There is another strong link between the world of the Early Stone or Hirsute Hips Age and modern times, namely a certain amount of sexual confusion. Swanscombe Man, as he is universally recognised, is in fact a woman. Palaeontologists are clever enough to be able to tell us, on the basis of half a skull, that she was young and buxom. Indeed, if hairy gals are your cup of tea, she was not unattractive. Exactly how she came to meet her end at so young an age is unclear. She may have drowned in one of the marsh inlets. She may have succumbed to one of the Estuary fevers, the agues that were still plaguing the region at the end of the nineteenth century. Or she may, at around 31, have grown too arthritic to escape the attentions of some beast that loved her for what she was, as a meal.

Did she have a husband, children, and a family? We can never know. But whatever her original fate, Swanscombe Girl has found a cosy enough billet in a glass case in the heart of the country where she once roamed. Here she lies, forever young, and yet the oldest person in the land.

As for Barnfield Pit, where she lay for 230,000 years, she would probably feel quite at home there now. The pit cuts down into geological strata far older even than Swanscombe Gal herself. It exudes wildness, danger and a pungent aroma. If this smell doesn't emanate from a set of functioning mammoth glands, it certainly suggests such a source. And, apart from some discarded snack packets and that crumbling "Danger – Keep Out" notice, it shows no signs at all that the world has moved on in the past 230 millennia. This, then, is the historic site that compares in significance with the Tower of London or the orchard where Isaac Newton discovered that apples don't float upwards when they drop off trees. There are no turnstiles or guidebooks, but the sense of raw neglect lends all the more power to Swanscombe Girl's one-time home.

Facing Barnfield Pit is a small cul-de-sac called Broomfield Road, with a few isolated grey concrete-clad houses scattered round it. We wandered up here to see how Swanscombe Girl's descendants were faring. Although it was summer, we shivered with cold. The wind whistled off the Estuary, then turned into Broomfield Road, shaking the dustbins as it went. Two boys were playing football under a council notice that read: No Ball Games. One house along, a man in overalls had stripped down an old van. It lay in pieces on his patch of front garden. Perhaps my head was a bit over-full of prehistoric thoughts concerning mammoths and New Stone Age types, but the vehicle suggested a dismembered elk. Perhaps it had something to do with the look of satisfaction on the proud face of the dismantler, vaguely suggestive of a Stone Age hunter who had brought home the meat. I felt in my pocket for my notebook, then thought better of it. I'd written enough for one day, and the world could do without an article on dismantled Transit vans.

So just for once I didn't introduce myself as a reporter. Instead, I just said: "Nice motor you've got there."

"Well, you need something reliable to get about in," the man agreed. "We're a bit isolated out here. Looks like you could use some wheels to get around in yourself," he said, looking at my rucksack. Then he must have caught me looking just a touch too intently at him. His tone changed. "Do you want something then?"

I shook my head hastily. I couldn't tell him the truth. What I had been looking at with such close interest was his skull.

It took just a few days for the story about the Queen Victoria statue to start spinning. The *Gravesend Messenger* published a full-page report. It did not go so far as to accuse the Southend Queen Victoria of filching this all-important item of Gravesend infrastructure, but the article was certainly couched in terms of cautious indignation. Southend Council responded with vehemence. "Hands off our hand," their spokesman exclaimed.

Essex Dog and I were interviewed on a number of local radio stations. "Of course, I do not go so far as to accuse Southend of making off with that hand, but …" I began each interview. Nobody wanted to spoil a good story, but eventually the new Southend hand was traced to a Shoebury sculptor, Jim Davis. He had quietly and without ballyhoo remade the Southend hand. He had even been paid for it out of the Council's missing hands budget. The whereabouts of the Gravesend Victoria's hand remains a mystery.

Inevitably, the interviewers got to enquiring as to just what an Essex boy thought he was up to, what with sticking his nose into Kentish affairs and sniffing round their disabled statuary. I told them about the Estuary Trail, figuring that it was, by this stage, far enough advanced. Even the swiftest and greediest rival rambler would not be able to catch up and claim it for his own.

"What is the point of this walk?" The question was asked, more than once. "Well, it's the biggest nature reserve in England," I said. "But also, there's something out there. You know, some sort of answer. Only I haven't got the question sorted out yet." This threatened to become unduly heavy, so the conversation was swiftly steered back to statues of Victoria and missing hands, things that anybody could relate to.

At the end of it all, I had to ask: just what good had it all done? Even on the other side of the water, I'd been incorrigible. I just couldn't stop digging up stories. Yet something had been achieved. It had been conclusively proved that there was life in Gravesend. It was no longer just a dim presence on the other side of the water. The heart of the town had been penetrated. A distant civilisation had been infiltrated. I felt like an honorary citizen of Gravesend. The feeling was accentuated when a number of people rang with suggestions as to where to look for the missing hand, some of them quite polite.

I went back to the statue of Victoria in Southend to look again at Her Majesty's new hand. One mystery had been solved, but another now presented itself. Ma'am's arm, complete with its restored appendage, is raised aloft, pointing quite forcefully at something out in the Estuary. But who or what is she indicating? Whatever the answer, it is something significant. Perhaps the thief who stole the original hand thought that it might lead him to the answer. A crock of gold? The secret of life? Or maybe, nothing as mystical as that, just a good walk that everybody ought to try.

The reality of the Thames Estuary – primeval, glutinous ooze

Coalhouse Fort

Nine

Dickens' Country

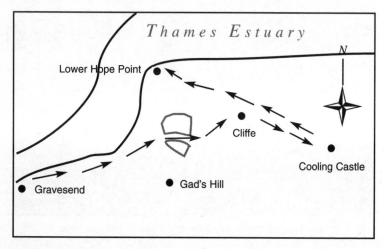

I HAD just about got used to the amenities of town-walking –
I even stopped to buy some salami, which is not something you
find on marshes or rubbish tips, and if you do, you don't want
to take it home. Then, yet again, the Estuary trail dropped us
into the middle of a wilderness.

The 25 square miles of marshland between Gravesend and
Allhallows have been described as "the largest tract of uninhabited land within twenty miles of Buckingham Palace,"
something HM the Queen will doubtless confirm if anyone
cares to ask. The flat land between the Estuary and the Kentish
hills is full of swans and sheep, but the human population registers as zilch. Behind the massive Thameside dykes lies a world
that is green and clean and regular. It is full of the sound of bird-
song, but not of the characteristic rasping cough of the human
species. It amounts to a green desert, 25 square miles of startlingly
unblemished chlorophyll. It is a naturalist's or hermit's paradise,
but a newspaperman or vacuum-cleaner salesman's worst nightmare.

Yet these lonely and untravelled marshes are anything but anonymous. They bear a famous name, and half the English-speaking world has stumbled across them some time, at least in the imagination. For this is the Dickens Country.

Charles Dickens moved here in 1856, to a house on Gads Hill, overlooking the marshes but safely out of sneering distance from all those swans. He had first passed this house (now a girl's school) when he was a child, on a Sunday afternoon walk with his father. In the words of Edgar Johnson, the young Dickens stared "with admiration at the rose and madder façade and drew a long breath of longing and incredulity when his father told him that if he were to work very hard he might come to live there one day." Courtesy of the dreams that he wove for millions of readers, Dickens' own dream came true. Here he lived for the last fourteen years of his life, and here he died, on 9 June 1870. The move from London to Gad's Hill is reflected in his novels. The marshland, with the foggy, haunted old cathedral town of Rochester as its capital, became the focus of his stories. He was no longer the great writer about London. He had moved upmarket and downriver. Charlie was an Estuary man now.

From the top floor of his beloved Gad's Hill Place, Dickens could look out over the marshes and Estuary, and he swiftly made this world his own. His presence pervades this world of mud, reeds and water not just as a writer, but as a fanatical walker. Most days he would embark on a short stroll around the neighbourhood. The term short stroll was a rare case of Dickens under-stating something. A "short stroll" for Dickens was a twelve-mile hike in anybody else's book. A short stroll with Dickens was bad news for any house-guest. More than once the Gad's Hill carriage had to be dispatched to scoop up Dickens' hiking companions, collapsed with exhaustion by the side of the road. But Dickens himself just kept on walking. In the process, he must have encountered some of the characters who people his last books. Some of his most outstanding character portraits hail from this period – Jasper the schizophrenic choir-master of *Edwin Drood*; Joe Gargary, one of the most convincingly "good" characters in literature; and the jilted, embittered bride Miss Havisham (both in *Great Expectations*). They are all people of the Dickens Country.

It is amazing how Dickens has colonised the world's imagination, even for those who've never read a word of one of his books (something, incidentally, they share with Dickens himself, who tended to be too busy either writing or carousing to find much time for reading, and certainly not for reading those huge long tomes by that Dickens fellow). During the period that Essex Dog and I walked the Dickens country, the word "Dickensian" appeared every day of the week in a national newspaper. David Copperfield dominated prime-time TV. Yobos in my own home town continued to congregate and brawl at the local low-dive, christened the Dickens, and bearing his features in a great big pub-sign, although the building is made from polystyrene and Dickens never came within twelve miles of the place. Yet his name was carefully selected. For some reason, the name Charles Dickens is reckoned to sell more lager. Charles Dickens' mugshot also, bizarrely, loomed above the financial reports on the 9 o'clock news, thanks to his presence on the old £10 notes. Or perhaps it was just an ironic comment by the BBC on the relation between economic forecasting and humorous fiction. Another remarkable thing about Charles Dickens: he is the only person on record to have bothered to row across the Thames for a night out on Canvey Island. All in all, he is a lot more alive, 130 years after his death, than many of today's dozy or drugged-up novelists.

Once he started to write at Gad's Hill, the focus of Dickens' novels moved away from London and into this God-forsaken, but not Dickens-forsaken, wilderness. Most famously, the opening scenes of *Great Expectations*, his most widely-read novel, are set on the marshes. The orphan Pip, living at the blacksmith's forge, hears the sound of cannon-fire. Out on the river are moored the rotting hulks of old sailing-ships. Within these foul floating slums lie thousands of convicts, waiting for transportation to Australia. The cannon-fire is a warning that one of these convicts has escaped. Pip's encounter with the convict in question, Magwitch, will be the key to all his future fortunes. One reads all novels from the modern angle, and the question I ask is this: Magwitch would prefer to spend his days waist-deep in mud on a frozen bog than head for Australia. Is this an early example of an anti-Aussie joke?

Essex, where Dickens barely set foot, uses him as a selling-point for lager. Yet over in his home country on the far side of the river, the Dickens link remains woefully unexploited. Not many stretches of countryside are fortunate enough to be adopted by a great writer. When such a thing does happen, the local population is usually quick to scent gold-dust. Entire local economies hinge on these literary links. Even within Thomas Hardy's own lifetime, the Hardy countryside, in Dorset, was moving from production of milk and beef into the spinning of Hardy Country tea-towels. Hundreds of Stratfordians make a living from Shakespeare. So much so that one Warwickshire schoolboy, asked to identify a picture of the Bard, is said to have answered: "Oh, that's my dad's boss." Even DH Lawrence now has his own Nottinghamshire Lawrence Country, known amongst the more disrespectful as the Randy Lands. The Dickens marshes, however, have failed to exploit their legendary aura. Maybe this is because a population of nil, by definition, does not include any publicity agents. Whatever the reason, it's a crying shame. What this Kentish countryside needed was a good dose of Essex barrow-boy business sense.

As it happened, not long beforehand, I had been talking to a restaurant proprietor. An uninhibited wide boy from a middle Eastern country, he had already made a fortune from themed restaurants in Essex locations. He owned a pub based on Dick Turpin, where the highwayman appeared, amongst his other fell deeds, to have stolen the barmaids' bras. My interviewee also ran a highly successful roadhouse based on a Mississippi river-boat. He was now anxious to expand onto the Kent shore. For he had got whiff of the Thames Gateway project.

The Thames Gateway is a massive government scheme to redevelop the north and south banks of the Estuary. It includes the prospect of a road-bridge carrying the A130 from Canvey Island to St Mary's Marsh. Thousands of houses, shops and factory units will be constructed at the Kent end of the bridge, all set to liven up those empty, fogbound, unproductive marshes.

"You are a local reporter who asks lots of questions. So now I ask you a question. You know the area. You tell me what is a good place for my next eatery," he said.

By now the Estuary had come to take over much of my mind space, waking and sleeping. I also owed a favour to someone who was desperately trying to find a home for a leaky Thames barge. So naturally I put in a bid on Old Man Thames' behalf. "What about a floating restaurant?" I suggested. "If you put out to sea at meal-times, nobody could slip away without paying their bill."

"Too risky," he said. "It sinks, people drown, I lose business. I have to pay divers to bring up the night's takings."

"Okay, so it doesn't have to put to sea at all," I said, rising to the challenge. "Just stick it on the mud and start to party. That's what most people do with their boats in Essex. They wouldn't be caught dead putting to sea."

"So what do we call this place. I tell you, it will not be called The Shrimp. No placed run by Ali is called The Shrimp." Even a sensibility as obtuse as mine could see that Ali had it in for restaurants called The Shrimp.

I had just seen David Lean's famous movie version of *Great Expectations*. I had Kent boglands on the brain. The answer seemed obvious. "Call your restaurant the Charles Dickens' Great Mastications," I told him. "Design it all up to look like a stinking prison hulk – you know, antique slop-buckets for the salad bar, that sort of thing. Dress all your waiters and waitresses in striped suits to look like Victorian convicts. It can't fail."

Ali said he'd think about it, and wished me a long and happy career in the local newspaper business. For some reason, perhaps not unconnected with the fact that he went out of business soon afterwards, he failed to take up this suggestion. But it seemed a shame to waste such a good idea. I had always harboured a faint ambition to run a restaurant when I retired, or was sacked, from journalism. My wife is a talented bouncer and the dog can clear a table of leftovers in seconds, so as a family we were well set up with the requisite skills. Even if the restaurant failed as a business proposition, any story about its setting up and development was guaranteed to run and run. And why, I mused, stop at just one little ship. A whole succession of vessels could link up. They could create the floating equivalent of a food-court in a shopping mall. The East Anglian coast is littered with mouldering historic vessels, and mouldering owners desperate to offload or at least find a use for them. I could picture them now – the old motor-torpedo boat, the floating Portuguese gambling salon at Maldon, the derelict cockle-fishing Dunkirk veteran, all making their way gratefully to the chosen site, and a new life in the catering business. Some of them were so mouldy that they might even sink on the way, creating further delicious headlines. Part of our mission on these lonely marshes, then, was to locate a suitable site for our mudbound hulks.

Alas, it didn't take long to dash our dreams. The empty landscape and the cold wind blowing in off the river soon imposed a dose of reality, just as they must have withered many a bright dream down the centuries. There was a fatal flaw in the scheme. However many hulks were gathered together to serve food and drink, however enthusiastically unemployed actresses might cavort around in convicts' stripes, there was nobody around to do the eating. The market wasn't there. Dickens' novels may teem with human life, but the Dickens country itself is deserted. Here and there are dotted the remains of dwellings, indicating that once upon a time, a few people eked out a living here, even if only by cleaning each others' windows. But even domesticity was always a bold idea too far here.

We had travelled through empty wastelands before on the Estuary trail. Foulness was a wilderness by anybody's standards. But on Foulness there was always a compensating factor. The place only *appeared* deserted. In reality, scores of secret agents were busily tapping out their memoirs in bunkers just a few inches beneath our feet. The Dickens Country is altogether different. There really is nobody around for miles. Nor is there any way to get a car up to the sea-wall, making a nonsense of the EC grant for building a restaurant car-park that I had applied for from Brussels. Indeed, the noise of the internal combustion engine was nowhere to be heard. The only form of motorised transport to venture anywhere near us was the occasional 30,000 ton ocean-going ship – and there was absolutely no chance of them heaving to at my restaurant for a quick bite.

From below the seawall, with the river itself invisible, these ships gave the odd impression of cruising through the fields. They made it look as if was easy to nurse a rig the size of a toppled office-block through the marshes. In fact, even walking can prove a dodgy process in places. At one stage, with my nose deep in the pages of *Great Expectations* as I walked, I missed the path and slid down the slope of a drainage ditch. I came to rest in a patch of nettles about two feet from the edge. For a moment, I pondered whether to slide in further. The mishap would have been worth at least 2,000 words. It could have occasioned a headline to die for: *Scandal of 5-hour rescue services: fire service slower than in Dickens' day*. But it was cold, and the mud stank, and I wasn't *that* dedicated. Perhaps we could find some rookie reporter to throw in the mud.

Consigning the Great Mastications restaurant chain to history as yet another lost cause of the Estuary, I started to look around for some sort of human interest story to enliven the miles. Dickens had discovered some outsize personalities on his walks hereabouts. Nothing very significant had happened since then to change the place or its people. There must, then, be some Dickensian characters out on these marshes. I pictured a tribe of great booming eccentrics, perhaps even dressed in Victorian costume (it was unlikely that news of the anorak had filtered through to the marshes yet). These undiscovered personalities could be shaken down for the stories they had to tell and their hilarious ways of telling them.

The plodding miles passed. But no human beings, outsize personalities or otherwise, made an appearance. After a few miles, my standards started to slip. Forget wandering Punch and Judy-men or shepherds in smocks. I would have settled for a monosyllabic drainage technician. But even he didn't put in an appearance. Deprived of humans, I had to make do with buildings. The seawall path took us past the Victorian gun-emplacements at Shornemead and Cliffe. I knew at least three military historians who went quite weak at the knees at mention of these artillery batteries. To the uninformed eye, however, they just appeared like large brick arches. Perhaps their most impressive feature is the graffiti. This is powerful enough, if flashed against the enemy, to be in breach of the Geneva Convention.

After four and a half miles, the Thames-side path hits a series of giant gravel-pits. The trail swings inland in a sweep round these pits, before rejoining the seawall below Lower Hope Point. In fact, we could have picked our way along the concrete tip of the seawall. But I knew that the stretch from there as far as Allhallows was the bleakest of all. The Gravesend marshes had been empty enough. But they were nothing compared with the deadlands that stretch along the misnamed Blythe Sands. There was absolutely no chance of finding a decent human-interest story over the next ten miles. So we left the river, and followed the trail inland, heading for the little hill-edge town of Cliffe. For a while we followed the edge of the gravel-pit. And it was on that that we at long last spotted our first Dickens character.

He wasn't wearing a frock-coat and pince-nez. He was wear-

ing a rubber wetsuit. He wasn't driving a mail-coach and horses. He was riding a wetbike. None of this mattered. He was a
marshland character whether he liked it or not. The gravel-pits
correspondent of *Evening Echo* required an interview. First the
man or woman – or with a bit of luck, the performing llama –
inside the rubber suit, had to be waylaid. This was no mean feat
when the potential interviewee in question was moving in high-
speed circuits round a submerged gravel-pit. Particularly if, as I
suspected, I was about to disrupt a world speed record attempt.
Standing on the edge, I flapped my arms and flashed my press-
card at his speeding figure. At first he failed to notice, or
ignored me. Eventually, with a spluttering of the engine, he
broke his circuit and came roaring up, bringing his wetbike to a
halt at my feet. He had hauled his helmet off even before he
stopped.

"Your little dog alright?" he asked, concernedly.

"Yeah, fine …

"You alright, mate?," he asked, with rather less concern.

"Yes, we're both okay. Look, I'm local press … well, sort of
local, for today, any rate. Just wanted to ask you a few questions, if you don't mind."

"Not the Old Bill then?"

"No …"

"They don't really like us here, you see," he explained. He
sounded surprisingly posh for a man by himself on a wetbike on
a gravel-pit on a weekday. "They've got all this water but they
don't want anybody playing with it for some reason."

"Are you a professional," I asked.

He laughed. "No. I just come here when I can. I sold my
business. You've got to do something with the time, haven't
you. Wife doesn't like me hanging round the house. Not that's
she's there much herself."

"You must see some things here, don't you," I asked,
eagerly.

"Things?"

"Well, bodies being dumped in the pit, mutated fish – odd things like that. Things that you get, er, excited about."

He gave me an odd look. "I've got to go now," he said. Hesitating for a moment, he suddenly reached into some rubber recess and fished out some money. "That little dog of yours looks like she could do with a square meal. Why don't you head up into the village and get us all a filled roll."

"We're not hungry at all," I said indignantly, showing him a packet of Polos I had in my pocket by way of proof. But he roared off on his wetbike in a way that allowed no further argument. That was the rather inconclusive end of my interview, but I didn't reckon it altogether a failure. A bored toff performing aimless, illegal high-speed circuits on a wetbike. A modern Dickens could have made a minor character, at least, out of that. It was also, somehow, a very Estuary occurrence.

As we trudged towards Cliffe, I made up my mind to take a detour. The Dickens marshes can boast one truly striking landmark, and one alone – the medieval castle at Cooling. It is the sole building that the local guidebooks bother to mention. Indeed, stuck for anything much else to discuss, local guides tend to dwell on the sheep – an interest that, in any other context, would be regarded as positively unhealthy. Photographs of the castle that I had seen certainly made it look impressive. Although much of it had been destroyed, there were still two soaring round towers, a mighty gatehouse and a swathe of curtain-wall enclosing the old keep – enough antique architecture to set Essex Dog howling for hours on end. Unlike Hadleigh Castle, it doesn't hug the water's edge. It stands two miles back from the Thames, at the edge of the downs. It is still a marshland castle, however, built to guard the Thames approaches against that old menace, garlic-breathing foreigners. It would make the ideal headquarters for the UK Independence Party.

Cooling Castle had an additional appeal for me, since it once housed my all-time fictional hero, or at least his real-life counterpart. Between 1410 and 1417, it was the home of Sir

John Oldcastle, the model for Shakespeare's Falstaff. Any political journalist will tell you that there is a clear connection between Oldcastle and Falstaff, because Shakespeare himself goes out of his way to deny that such a link exists – "Oldcastle died a martyr, and this is not the man," he declares. He had been leant on rather heavily by Oldcastle's family. If this isn't enough proof, he also chose a local setting for one of Falstaff's finest hours. Gad's Hill lies just behind Cooling Castle. In Henry IV Part I, the old rogue attempts to rob some merchants, then runs away when the going gets too hot. The setting is Gad's Hill. Four centuries later, Dickens arrived to take up residence on the exact spot, thus providing an odd link between our two greatest writers.

On the path to Cooling Castle, I bored myself with reminiscences about how I once played the seventeenth ostler in an amateur production of *The Merry Wives of Windsor*. I had been granted the memorable line: "Rhubarb, rhubarb, horses, horses, rhubarb, rhubarb." With little to worry about in terms of missed cues or forgetting my lines, I was left with plenty of time to observe the onstage frolics of Falstaff. The life-loving, sack-swilling, big-bellied lecherous old coward has been role model No 1 ever since. It has always been my ambition to play him on stage, although to date the nearest I have got is the leap from seventeenth to fifteenth ostler.

Just beyond Cliffe, I felt in my pocket and came across the money that the wetbike rider had given me to buy lunch for the dog and himself. There was £2.50, enough for two buns and a sausage roll for the dog. I had no intention of retracing my footsteps at this late stage. But how long before my benefactor realised that he wasn't going to get his lunch? Could he hear his own tummy rumbling, somewhere inside that wetsuit? Would he call the police? And if so, how did they operate on the marshes? Would £2.50 worth of missing bun-money justify the launching of the police helicopter? Or would I be pursued across the Dickens Country by the boys in blue, also on wetbikes? Either way, suddenly, I knew how Magwitch the convict felt.

One mile south-east of Cliffe we arrived at the supposed site of Cooling Castle. There was, however, no sight of anything that resembled a castle. True, the search was made more diffi-cult by the need to hug the hedgerows and keep to the shadows – I was on constant alert for police sharpshooters. It was only when Essex Dog began to whimper that I knew she had dis-covered, not the dead badger she had been digging for, but something medieval.

It was just a fragment of flint wall, but from here we were able to pick up the line of the castle's defences. This led us at last to the gatehouse and twin towers, hugging a narrow lane. Yet in one sense, the mystery deepened. While Essex Dog howled, and begged to be led away from the scene, I pondered why anybody should want to build such a thing as a reticent castle. All the other castles I had ever seen had been show-off, egregious things, built to make their presence felt, to awe any enemies, tower above a cowed peasantry, and generally deter any unpleasantness. Hadleigh, the other medieval Estuary cas-tle, was a case in point. Its great towers and turrets are assem-bled on the Thames side. Any sensible sea-raider, setting eyes on this particular fortress, would mutter: "Stone me, size does matter, I'm out of here!" Cooling Castle, by contrast, for all its soaring towers, had done its best to remain invisible. It was tucked into the lee of a hill, not stuck on top for all to see, and masked by large trees and the folds in the ground. So concealed is Cooling that a short-sighted rambler could easily collide with it. Added to this, all the stoutest defences are mustered, not along the Estuary side, but along the quiet, inland country lane to the south, facing into Kent. Natural enemies, be they French pirates or history-hating dogs from Essex, would approach from the Estuary. Yet this side was protected only by an unimpressive curtain-wall.

Seizing his chance, the irksome little landscape detective Sherlock Roams promptly popped up from the dead once again.

Roams had been tried out as a newspaper feature, ignored by readers, and consigned to the bin, all in the course of four weeks. But he wouldn't lie down.

"So you want to solve the mystery of the hidden castle. Very well, apply the methods I have taught you, my dear King."

"Go fall off a waterfall."

He was not to be deterred, alas. "If you are not prepared to do the thinking for yourself, I will just have to do it for you," he announced, dodging the buckshot from a mental elephant gun that I promptly discharged at him. "Now, if Cooling Castle is hidden, it follows that it was intended to be hidden. The purpose, was it not, was surprise. The French raiders who laid waste the marsh country in 1380 found themselves unopposed. When they returned the following year, they would have been lulled into a false sense of security. Unable to see any castle, they would assume that none was there. Suddenly, when they least expected it, an entire garrison would descend upon them from nowhere.

"If I may be permitted to paraphrase Corporal Jones in Dad's Army, there is nothing that a French warrior likes less than a twelve-foot pike up him. It becomes considerably more galling if he cannot even see where that pike is coming from."

Much to my relief, a twelve-foot pike at this stage found its mark in Sherlock Roams, and he disappeared with a hurt squeak. Irritating though he was, however, it had to be admitted that his argument carried some weight. But whys and wherefores were beside the point. The fact was, I had discovered the great selling point of the Dickens Marshes. Where else can you miss a castle that is right under your nose? Commentators have dwelt on technical aspects of Cooling Castle, such as its early examples of gun-ports, while missing the most bizarre aspect of the place. Somebody had gone to immense trouble to hide a castle, towers and all. It was the opposite of the "if you've got it, flaunt it" approach. But Cooling's builder was an Estuary man, infected with Estuary principles. "Conceal your virtues" would have been a more appropriate motto for him. The Thames Gateway people had been desperate for some sort of tourist focus, and here it was – the lost castle of Cooling. What better icon for the gateway to London?

Set into the gateway of Cooling Castle is a plaque. It declares, in rather self-righteous terms, how Cooling Castle was built for the defence of the realm. It says: "I am mad in help of the culture." Translation: I am made in help of the country. Yet was the word "mad" such a mis-spelling? The Old hack's cynicism and long experience of hidden agendas popped up at this stage. Didn't a hidden castle fit everything that we knew about John Falstaff? Sieges and sallies waste good drinking and wenching time. Those magnificent towers face towards the village. They were well placed to defend the castle against the bloodiest enemies of all. Forget the French. The real danger came from the likes of debt-collectors, would-be mothers-in-law, and burglars bent on filching the wine from a chap's cellars. Safe behind those huge towers, the original of Sir John Falstaff could have caroused the days and nights away, without fear of disruption. Only the intuitive genius of Shakespeare managed to penetrate those walls, and capture the wild nights and drunken japes that went on there.

Or is this unfair to dedicated and professional soldiers, whose only interest lay in protecting their country? Maybe. But the one item of paperwork to survive from the building of Cooling suggests a different story. It is a letter from the castle architect, protesting that he hasn't been paid. Did he become one of those debt-collectors, beating at the doors that he himself had built? Whatever the truth, Essex Dog and I shared a celebratory Polo, in memory of those castle inhabitants, as mysterious as the hidden castle itself.

With some sense of foreboding, we headed back through Cliffe and out towards the loneliest stretch of the walk. I had the

£2.50 that my wetbike friend had given me, ready to return to him. There had been no sign of any bread-rolls for sale in the little town, but I had purchased him a packet of cheese-and-onion crisps, with my own money, by way of compensation. But the gravel-pit was deserted. There was neither sight nor sound of wetbike or rider. No doubt he was even now hammering the desk at Rochester police station and reporting the theft of his lunch by a disreputable tramp posing as a journalist, and his pet rat. Involving, as it did, a craft on gravel-pit waters, would this count as piracy, rather than the less severe offence of aggravated theft?

Our fears were made worse by a sinister discovery. Alongside the gravel-pit, we came across the burnt-out remains of a motor-bike. Such sites can provide rich pickings for scavengers, so we stopped for a rummage. Cars that have been abandoned and burnt out by joyriders have provided, amongst other items, a genuine Ford Cortina nameplate and a perfectly toasted sandwich. After a few seconds poking among the ashes, however, I realised that this was no burnt-out motorbike. It was a burnt-out wetbike. For one terrible moment, I wondered whether it was the one that had belonged to our friend. Weakened from hunger, had he crashed into the bank of the gravel-pit? Then clear sense dawned. The wreck was several weeks old.

This scarcely improved our prospects. As wandering con-men from Essex, the types who would trick an honest Kentish speed-merchant out of his lunch, we were also bound to come under suspicion as the boy-racers who had taken the wetbike. The sense of unease spread to the dog, normally a fan of fast vehicles – especially wrecked ones, which tend to stink better. Now all she wanted to do was put some ground behind us. One step ahead of the law, we hastened into the ever wilder marsh country. There we would be safer. We knew the police would be too scared to pursue us, and anyway their overtime allowance wouldn't stretch to covering the chase. It was a landscape so forlorn that even the word Dickensian was inadequate to describe its grimness.

The fog rolled off the river and filled the streets of the old city. It was so cold that even the hot-chestnut sellers had left the street. Or perhaps, sick of the chill, they had decided to re-train indoors as computer programmers. Nothing had really changed since Charles Dickens described this scene in the 1830s: "Water is a perverse sort of element at the best of times, and in Mudfog (Rochester) it is particularly so," wrote the master. "It *will* turn green, and although green is a very good colour in its way, especially in grass, still it certainly is not very becoming in fog." In these audio-distorted surroundings, you could hear heels ringing on cobblestones one hundred yards away, hear the coughing-fits of the citizens of Rochester echoing round the ancient medieval courtyards. Cold and miserable as it was, the fog suited the conspiratorial nature of my quest.

Some months had passed since we had scuttled as fast as we could across the Dickens marshes. Now I had returned to Kent, this time by motor-car. I was engaged on a covert operation. The mission was to penetrate the Dickens Fellowship.

Ostensibly, the Dickens Fellowship meets in venues around the country to celebrate and discuss the work of Charles whatshisname. Suspicions had emerged, however, that this was a mere front.

The tip-off had come a few months beforehand. The scene had been the Mayor's parlour in Southend, and the man mouthing his suspicions was the honorary secretary of a local cookery club. "You should investigate that lot," he said. "I'm telling you, the Dickensians are on the march. They're muscling in on our territory, for starters. Poaching our venues and our dates with the Mayor. You make some enquiries. You'll be surprised what you find."

People are always saying: "you should investigate that." The targets range from funny noises in the house at two in the morning, to south Essex solicitors glimpsed in airports clutching one-way tickets and large rustling suitcases. Nine times out of ten such remarks are ignored, particularly one like this, which just reflected the familiar patterns of jealousy, rivalry and empire-building among local leisure clubs and societies. This one, however, was more useful, since it provided an excuse to infiltrate the Dickens Fellowship.

The journey across the Dickens marshes had proved something of a disappointment. Contrary to expectations, the wetlands had not been crawling with Dickens characters or Victorian atmosphere, or anything much else come to that, with the exception of container-ships. I was curious to know whether the spirit of Dickens lived on at all among local people. Where better to investigate than in Dickens' own hometown of Rochester, the city where he desired to be buried (he ended up in Westminster Abbey). This was what I really wanted to discover. To this end, I had shadowed Bernard Mason, the president of the Southend branch of the Dickens Fellowship, on one of his regular trips across the Estuary. According to my expenses form, I was there to unearth any Dickensian dirty-doings that might become apparent. But my real purpose, the secret agenda to the secret agenda, I suppose, was to discover whether Dickens could be infectious. Did people still continue to act like Dickens characters when they lived at the spiritual centre of Dickens country?

In order to blend in and look as inconspicuous as possible, I had dressed in early Victorian style. By the time the wardrobe was complete, I reckoned that I bore a pretty good likeness to Mr Boffin, the rubbish-heap proprietor in *Our Mutual Friend*. I stood at the entrance to the Rochester Assembly Rooms, waiting for the Dickensian fanatics to emerge out of the shadows and alleyways in all their period finery.

People were coming off the street alright, but they didn't look in the least bit Victorian. Most of them were wearing clothes from Next or Monsoon, others had jeans. Around seventy people passed through the Assembly Room doors while I watched. Mr Dickens still had drawing power alright. Many of the Dickensians threw me a curious glance, while trying not to appear too obvious. I was totally inappropriately dressed for the occasion. I had betrayed my lack of Dickensian breeding. One could only hope and pray that no social diarists were present tonight. Running back to the car, I threw a raincoat over the costume and scuttled back. The meeting of the Rochester branch of the Dickens Fellowship was just beginning.

Something big was in the air. The Dickensians were on the verge of their centenary. The announcement of "A big new project" was promised. I licked my pencil and my lips in antici-pation. The early proceedings, however, were oddly colourless. The society was run with brisk efficiency, its finances were in enviable shape, the minutes of previous meetings neatly record-ed. There were no headlines to be had from any of this. Still, the mere fact that the society was in such good trim suggested a hungry organisation that was all set to gobble up other, weak-er clubs. Was this the scandalous truth about the Dickens Fellowship – that it was just very successful, because the world was full of Dickens fanatics?

Things livened somewhat when the speaker stood up. His subject was Holes, Tunnels and Caves of the Locality. "People in this area get very excited about holes," he announced. The stir that he was making amongst the audience confirmed this. He then proceeded to explain how he had once spent three weekends digging beside a car-park in Chatham for a hole that turned out not to be there, though, of course, he did create his own hole as he looked.

I suddenly realised that there was an odd omission. We were one hour into the meeting, and the name Dickens had barely been mentioned. The speaker, true, had made passing reference to him. "I've only read one book by Dickens," he'd said. Somehow, at some stage, the Rochester Dickens Fellowship appeared to have mutated into the Rochester Federation of

Diggers. Now I merely had to discover just what they were digging for and I would have my story. Was it buried treasure? State secrets? Or did the passion for hole-digging on the marshes go right back to poor, unfortunate Swanscombe Man and his desperate attempt to become a caveman?

But the key to the story, as it turned out, didn't lie in any hole, but in something even more basic.

Of course. Food.

The branch chairman stood to announce the launch of the project: a book called Drink & Drive with Dickens. The plan was ambitious – a countrywide eat-in covering all the surviving watering-holes where Charles Dickens himself had consumed a meal or drunk a tot. If the hostelry offered a slice off an aged Stilton that could personally remember Dickens' visit, so much the better. But even fresh food would justify a mention in the book that would cover all these visits.

It suddenly dawned on me just how many pubs along the Estuary trail could make it into print. The Britannia at old Southend, the Lobster Smack at Canvey, the Peter Boat at Leigh, the World's End at Tilbury and the Three Daws at Gravesend, all claimed Dickensian status. Indeed, it was a wonder that such a dedicated pub-crawler ever got any work done.

The smacking of lips, the patting of paunches and all the other signs of appreciation, not to mention the scramble for entry forms, was a sight to behold. Here, at last, was the true spirit of Dickens at work, as the club-members prepared to confront their vittals. Somehow or other, there was a form in my hand, too.

Then the meeting was over. The Dickensians dispersed into the murk. The night was getting old, and it was a long way home. Yet what happened next was irresistible. I drove carefully through the fog to Allhallows, alighting at the ancient hostelry of The Rose & Crown, close by the Estuary trail. I ordered a pint of ale, studied the menu, and began to take notes. Competitive instincts were emerging. I had come to spy on the militant Dickensians, and ended up by joining their ranks. So be it. In that case, I was going to be first to file my report.

Sitting beside the pub's bow-window, I looked out toward the river, and the Estuary trail, now invisible in the darkness. Then I scratched a few notes for the Drinking with Dickens Guide. "Rose & Crown: sixteenth century tavern in old Allhallows village, in Dickens' lifetime, the first and last pub on the Great Marsh. Its warm lights, shining through the two bow windows, must have come as a welcome relief for any traveller ..." I paused for a moment, recalling the long, lonely trek of that summer, then added: "or persons with other business on the marshes."

On a foggy night, the Dickens marshes look inviolate enough, and sufficiently powerful to resist any intruder. Yet their days are probably numbered, as the homes, factories and roads of the Thames Gateway project spread across them.

Perhaps, though, the marshes don't completely lack for friends after all. The feisty spirit of Charles Dickens lives on around the Estuary, after all. The Dickensians are on the march, and the Lord help anybody who gets in their ... I mean, our ... way.

The large, unmarked, featureless turnip field at West Tilbury that was the site of one of the golden moments of English history

The best available monument, waiting for a beachcomber of the future

Ten

Allhallows – Thames Ghost-Town

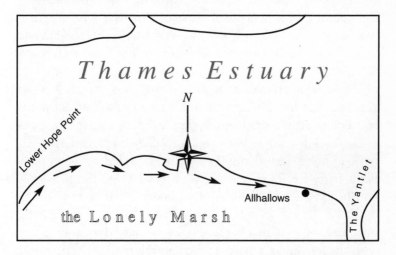

ON AND ever on we pressed, into the desolate lands. At Lower Hope Point, the Thames suddenly widened from what was still recognisably a river into an inland sea, the Thames Ocean. On the far side of the Estuary, the oil refineries, so vast to the eye on the Essex shore, had diminished into piddling pinpricks. We were voyaging into empty waters, even though we were on land. The last signs of human influence vanished. The wild country inland from us was also a sea, vast in its flatness and emptiness. Even a gravel pit or a discarded sofa would have been a welcome sight, almost a comfort for the little suburban creature that I was, stunned by the power of wilderness.

To add to the tension, I was by no means sure that I had any right to be on the seawall. There was a fine, clear path on top of it alright, grazed clear of weeds by the shy dinosaurs that clearly came out at night from the depths of this primeval wilderness. The Ordnance Survey map, however, did not indicate it as a footpath, although this was probably because their surveyors had never ventured this far into the dark lands. Even if we were trespassing, I would have quite welcomed the chance to be thrown off. With luck, some drainage big-shot would soon be bellowing: "Get off my wall!" through a megaphone, from the platform of a helicopter. At least this would be a sign of humanity. And with any luck, I could borrow his megaphone and get in a quick interview with him before I was thrown off the marsh.

There were animals enough in plenty. Sheep grazed in the gaps between the drainage ditches. At least one family of swans had colonised the drainage ditches. And, of course, the gulls circled and dived over the water, screeching imprecations. I felt quite at home with them; their noise reminded me of a Friday night party for some reporter who was leaving the provinces and heading for London. And, of course, thanks to the long deceased seagull Skeet, I knew just what that screeching meant. They were making that noise because they were fed up with the loneliness, whatever the naturalists might contend. "I know how you feel, fellas," I called.

The big ships also came across as a sort of animal, quite independent of mankind. A mile or two back, they had cruised close enough to the seawall for us to wave to their crews, those anyway who weren't tucked up in their cabins with their Playstations. But at Lower Hope, the ships moved far out into the centre of the Estuary. Now, as they moved slowly and silently through the haze, they seemed as remote as ghosts, genuine stately beings from another dimension as opposed to the odd-balls conjured up by Crystalbelle and her ilk. Still, I understood now why this uncanny inland sea seemed to spawn so many professed psychics and UFO-watchers along its shores.

"On and on they pressed, into the desolate lands." The line came from some politically incorrect adventure story about big white hunters that I had read as a child. I would read stories like that, then stare out over the Estuary, imagining myself with a Mauser for shooting villains and a pith-helmet to ram over the head of over-talkative society women, exploring darkest Africa. I never dreamed, though, that the journey I would make when I eventually packed my pith-helmet would be along the very horizon I was looking at, or that the bush country began just four miles south of home.

The sense of loneliness became so overpowering that I pondered whether to call somebody, anybody, on my mobile phone. My wife was busy and the Samaritans had more urgent cases to deal with than lonesome ramblers. But Directory Enquiries would be better than nothing. They at least should offer the sound of a human voice.

My finger was almost poised on the button when I at last glimpsed my Man Friday – two of him, in fact.

They were two scruffily dressed men in their early twenties. They had a generally listless demeanour about them, yet they were putting a lot of physical effort into what they were doing. This consisted of pitching rocks and pebbles as far out to sea as they could manage. It must have been some sort of competitive game. But the aggressive way in which they were hurling the missiles gave the impression that the passing ships had done something to infuriate them, and they were stoning the portholes in revenge.

Anybody who had actually chosen to make their way to this lonely place just had to have some sort of story to tell, so I rambled up to them at high speed, notebook in hand. They stared at me apprehensively.

"Name's King. *Evening Echo.* Local newspaper. Doing an 83-mile walk around the Estuary. Seen anything interesting while you've been out here?"

One of the men looked miserably at me. "Egg zug gum," he said.

"What?"

He looked hopelessly at his friend. They exchanged a few words in a language I couldn't even identify, let alone try to translate.

"Ag sile yum," said the second man. It sounded like the same word with different pronunciation.

A sudden thought dawned on me: "Are you Serbo-Croat, then, mate?" I asked him. "A mate of mine spoke Serbo-Croat. He got lots of work. Not on English local newspapers, of course."

There was something in what I said, possibly the word Serbo, that made them both bristle. The first man jabbered at me in his strange language. He sounded cross. Then he stopped his incomprehensible talking and indicated in unmistakeable sign language that I should get going.

"Oh, alright," I said, with an obtuseness cultivated over many years. "But how about a photograph first?"

They didn't want their picture in the paper, either, so I did what they suggested and started to walk on. After 150 yards, I turned round and waved at them. They were staring after me, but made no effort to wave back. For all their surliness, I rather missed these two guys as the Estuary desert gathered round me once again.

It occurred to me as I walked along that one of them, at least, had appeared quite wet. Perhaps he'd been for a dip. But fully clothed? Maybe, perhaps, he came from some country where all the swimming-trunks had to be exported, to balance the national debt. You don't get to learn much about foreign countries in the restricted world of English provincial papers, but I reckoned that there were such places.

Or was it possible that they had jumped ship? There and then I realised what that word "egg zug gum" meant. It might have sounded like a sauce you pour over a cheap takeaway to disguise the taste, but in fact the word was English. The word was "asylum".

Two asylum-seekers on a seawall, vaguely trying to sink supertankers with pebbles. The only human life in this wilderness. But who or what were they trying to gain asylum from? Had they just escaped from some hellish foreign inferno? Or was the country that they were trying to escape from, with their plaintive plea for asylum, the country where they actually were. Were they begging to get away from the spirit-crushing desolation of the Thames marshes, to find refuge in some more amenable place, like the Balkans?

On and on we pressed, into the desolate lands. And then, suddenly, we stumbled on the last thing that we expected to find out here – a town. The little place lay in the most unlikely of places, surrounded by marsh. It was tiny. Unlike most towns in this day and age, when *urbs* guzzle everything in sight, it also looked frail and on its last legs. The Estuary country stood poised to re-invade at any moment. This was Allhallows.

We knew that Allhallows lay ahead, but, true to form, it arrived about one hour earlier than expected. Timing is one of many things that Allhallows always managed to get wrong.

Allhallows should appeal to anybody with a partiality for lost causes. It can be said, with some conviction, that causes don't come much more lost than Allhallows. I looked hard at the place for a few minutes, then made a note to check whether Oxford, the world centre of lost causes, had a Lost Cause Society. They might want to send a charabanc down here for the annual club outing.

It doesn't matter where you come from, whether by boat, or by foot across the marshes; you can look at it from whatever angle you choose; the fact is that Allhallows occupies one of the most godforsaken locations of any town in England. From the look of things, even double-glazing salesmen haven't found their way here yet. It only looks vaguely romantic when you view it from the Essex shore, on a bright day, when the sun reflects off the satellite aerials.

I suspect that the few outsiders who do arrive here, perhaps because they've followed a map of England purchased from a street-stall in Boulogne, don't even realise that they've arrived at somewhere that is a place, as such. This is the beginning of the great swathe of caravan-ville that marks the final stage of the Thames Estuary on the Kent shore. Tucked away and out of sight of the seafront is a small church without many graves. Residents can boast that not many people die in Allhallows (but then, not many people live there). There is also the Rose & Crown tavern, more marshland refuge than village inn. And that, almost, is blink-and-you-miss-it Allhallows for you. Yet Allhallows' seafront tells an altogether different and more ambitious story.

Between the caravan parks and the sea stand two buildings that belong to another world. They are a huge 1930s pub, the British Pilot, and a faded Art Deco apartment block that looks more like a seducer's pad in downtown Los Angeles than something stuck on the mud in the middle of English nowhere. They were such weird curiosities that I instantly set out to find out more about them.

I mentioned Allhallows to a Maid of Kent of my acquaintance. She was incredulous. "You're walking all those miles to get to Allhallows!" said my wife, for it was she.

"It's what this walk is all about," I replied defensively. "It's another of those places I've been staring at all my life but never set foot in."

"Well, I've been there," she point scored, but then lost all her points by saying she wished she had never done so. She then told me about her childhood memories of Allhallows, which saved me the bother of interviewing any strangers.

When she was young, her parents would say things like: "It's a lovely hot day. I know, let's go to the seaside at lovely Allhallows."

They were then rather surprised when their seven-year-old burst into tears. A child that didn't want to go to the seaside on a hot day? There must be something wrong with her. But there was nothing wrong with her. She just remembered things from her last visit. Little matters such as the deep mud into which she sank up to her waist; the great expanse of grey estuary that just seemed to get greyer, however sunny it was; the dullness of the little caravan townlet; and the puzzling lunacy that had taken over normally sane members of the human race, as they pretended that all this was somehow fun. Allhallows had flopped again.

If Allhallows really is so worthless, why not allow it to slumber in obscurity, instead of going on about it at such length? The answer is that you cannot ignore it. It hogs one of the prime sites on the Estuary, at the junction of the Yantlet Channel and the Thames. The lure goes beyond that, however. Anybody who knows the Allhallows story will find it fascinating. It is the fascination, once again, of failed dreams, the biggest of all the failed dreams of the Estuary. Once, long ago, people like the members of the Tilbury Action Group dreamed up a spectacular future for this outpost. The block of flats and the British Pilot are the remains of that future. The future has become history. In its way, Allhallows, lost, unknown, unvisited and possibly not even subject to British Summer Time, is a sort of figurehead for the Estuary.

Other countries treat their sea approaches with mighty monuments. Think of New York and the Statue of Liberty. Think of Athens and the Temple to Poseidon. England has made its gesture with Allhallows caravan park.

It might all have been so different. Just after World War I, a number of powerful parties, including Kent County Council and the London County Council, set out to transform Allhallows into the most magnificent seaside resort in the northern hemisphere.

Allhallows would become the swishiest of resorts, Miami or Nice on Thames, although without all the pesky sunshine. Above all, the place would outshine Southend, that booming, swinging, lit-up Essex metropolis whose lights winked at the empty Kent coast from the other side of the Estuary.

"Southend has grown from a row of fishermen's cottages into a prosperous conurbation in the course of less than a century," argued the developers. "Why should not the same process ensue at Allhallows, given vision and investment?"

Among the plans for Allhallows were the largest swimming-pool in Britain, along with the first artificial wave system in Europe, an amusement-park "four times the size of the famous one at Blackpool", and a town of four and a half square miles.

They got some way towards developing their dream, as well. They started by building a railway line, then added the British Pilot pub, and that block of flats to house the first wave of dedicated, pioneer drinkers.

The words of the prospectus were zestful enough. By contrast, the developers became uncharacteristically uneffusive when it came to accounting for why Allhallows failed to take off beyond this stage. It appears, however, that the world at large took the same attitude to Allhallows-on-Sea as my wife. The mere prospect of a day-trip there was enough to set them howling. Nobody turned up to enjoy the resort.

So the railway line was pulled up and the land allocated for expensive flats was given over to caravans instead. And Southend's lights continue to mock their dark, would-be opposition on the far side of the water.

Yet standing on one of the failed and unloved beaches, I realised – and accuse me of attention-seeking if you wish – that I had a soft spot for Allhallows. For one thing, it must be one of the few places that it is easier to ramble than motor to. The ten-mile walk from Gravesend seems less demanding than the endless criss-cross country drive through the Hoo peninsula needed to get a pint at the Rose & Crown.

For another, Allhallows provided the first hint of journey's end on the Estuary walk. The Ness of Shoebury had suddenly come into view on the far side of the water, beyond the shipping channel.

From this faraway vantage point, Southend doesn't look like "a prosperous conurbation" at all. It appears mysterious and even frail. It must be like seeing the town from a satellite in near space. All that teeming life, all those politics, the seafront crowds and the million commuter journeys, are reduced to a few distant, dreamy turrets and rooftops, dwarfed by the vastness of the Estuary. And on this side, I could see the curve of Sheppey Island, as it rounded the last bend to journey's end.

Allhallows may never have made it in a worldly sense, but in the way it exudes the essence of the Estuary, it is still unmatched. Maybe it's not such a failure after all.

History-hating Essex Dog picks her way nervously through Shoebury's old Horseshoe Barracks, now a ghost-town

Oil refineries spread for four miles along the Essex shore, deliberately designed to make life as difficult as possible for ramblers. The marshes, in the foreground, are no soft option either

Eleven

Sheppey – World's End

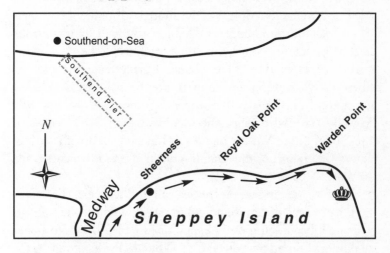

AS ANY jobbing psychologist will tell you, most people in the world have a special island of the mind. It is usually a rather vaguely defined one, and almost always inaccurately conceived. It may be a tropical paradise wafted with the scent of ripe iguanas, or it may be some remote, storm-lashed Hebridean outpost, populated solely by thirty spinster lighthouse-keepers whose subscription to *Rough Cheesecake* magazine has just expired. For those who actually make it in real life to their dream island, the reality is likely to be a tottering economy, a plague of sandflies, and – especially these days – a tidal wave strong enough to deter even the most determined loafer. Call me Charley Cynical, but all too often an island can be defined geographically as an area of disillusion entirely surrounded by water.

On the other hand, if a muddy mound called Sheppey, sinking into the Estuary under the weight of caravans, is your particular dream, then the chances are that reality can only improve on expectations. A taste for Sheppey, at least from a safe distance away, was something that I shared with at least one other person of my acquaintance. Shane Frome had seen it as a refuge, from wives, debtors and planning officials. He had tried to wade across to it, via the shortest distance. I had seen it as a distant, dim blur, shrouded not so much by mysterious mist as by mud vapour – yet still containing some sort of discovery or revelation. Like Shane, I had made my bid for Sheppey, albeit using the wimp's route, by walking 83 miles to get there. In order to arrive where we now stood, we had had to walk a second Estuary, the Medway, along sixteen miles of the Saxon Shore Way. It might not have equated with wading across the mouth of the Thames, but it showed dedication for all that.

Now I was standing on the seawall at Sheerness, the "capital town" of my dream island, taking stock. Did I really want to become a beach-bum on Sheppey, or just take the train home to dinner? I raised my palms to the Thames Estuary, waiting for some sort of reply, but as usual it didn't bother. Even without its help, it was possible to make a decision using a simple process of logic. The beach was conspicuously lacking in open-air cocktail bars, and the chances of a stranger cadging a regular salary off the *Daily Telegraph* readers walking their dogs on the beach looked slim. Beach bumming here would be no soft option.

Sheppey had already come up with at least one surprise, but it was an old surprise. The dog and I had spent the morning yomping through wild marshland, pining once again for human company. Whatever our expectations of Sheppey, they had never encompassed so much remoteness. There had been plenty of sheep, but even sheep can become a touch tedious after, oh – pluck a figure from the air ... five seconds. Flocks of Brent geese had honked the words: "Call that a dog?" as they flew overhead. Even these coarse beasts were company of a sort, but one flock of Brent geese tends to look and honk pretty much like another flock of Brent geese after a while. Essex Dog and I had supped our fill of wilderness, Estuary style. Now we were in search of novelty for the last few miles of this walk.

Novelty was not something we were likely to find in the town of Sheerness. We had checked it out, noting the Victorian clock-tower (its one landmark) and the Social Security office, just in case we did decide to take the beach-bum idea seriously. Sheerness was more prosperous and less dishevelled than I remembered from my last trip, nineteen years before. Far from being a raw Estuary outpost, it seemed a trim, confident little town, conveying no sense of its lonely location. And the clock on the clock-tower actually worked, at least when – having checked that no worthy local burgers were watching – I gave it a good kick.

This disappointingly pleasant little town was also, clearly, in constant terror of the Estuary. It has built a vast wall to keep the prowling beast at bay. This wall is a monumental achievement in its own right, but it does block Sheerness off from the sea as surely as any theatre fire-curtain separates audience from stage. You can almost touch the sea before you see the sea. In the past, this probably suited Sheerness people, whose economy revolved around the Queenborough docks (built by Samuel Pepys, of diary fame, and sycophantically named after the queen consort Catharine of Braganza, who never bust her arse operating a dockyard crane in her life). The people of Sheerness spent their working days around the briny. The last thing they wanted to do in their leisure time was to look at the thing. The phrase "sea views" probably knocked ten per cent off the price of a house.

Even Sheerness's attempt to turn itself into a seaside resort was always rather half-hearted. On my last visit, I had strolled through the shabbiest seaside fairground that I had ever encountered. The paint was peeling off the old wooden attractions, and the camels and horses on the roundabout all suffered from mange and foot & mouth. True, I did admire the giant model of the Leaning Tower of Pisa, until I realised that it wasn't a model of the leaning tower of anything, but the fairground helter-skelter. Now even these peeling gestures to seaside jolli-ty had gone, replaced by a spick-and-span Tesco.

It didn't matter that Sheerness was so unexciting, because today was Estuary day with a vengeance. The intent was clear-cut. We were going to stick to the hemline of the sea, resisting the blandishments of Sheppey's interior. Such siren calls were not to be scoffed at. They included the medieval abbey at Minster, built by the wonderfully named abbess Sexburgha. But leer and wink as she might, Sexburgha couldn't entice *me* away from the straight and narrow, let alone the dog.

The Estuary shore was my pathway, and the Estuary was my land, my glimpse of God's country, even if I couldn't plough or plant it. Some weeks beforehand, the dog and I had walked the edge of the Cotswold escarpment. On a clear, bright day we had looked out over a thousand meadows to the silver, glittering Severn, and, beyond that, to the Malvern Hills. And all we could think was: "It's lovely, but it's not the Thames Estuary – I want to go home."

So, how to explain away this Estuary love to a detached observer – or, indeed, to my own more rational side? On first impressions, it appeared ridiculous. The Estuary was no con-ventional beauty. Standing here on the sea-wall at Sheerness, the most obvious word that came to mind was: Dump. Not as a noun so much, rather as a forceful verb. So we need a dirty great power station to light up London, but nobody in Stepney wants the thing on their doorstep. Not to worry, little ol' Whitehall know just the place. Nobody in the Estuary will object; they'll just welcome the employment. *Dump.* So where do we find the space to store London's torrent of rubbish – the Millennium Dome? Nah, but there's unlimited space on the Estuary. *Dump.* We need a new airport, but those specks 10,000 feet below our aircraft don't want to become runway fodder. Never mind, nobody lives in the Estuary. *Dump.* It was easy, now, to understand why the nation's army of trailblazers had so signally failed to create an Estuary trail, and left it to me and

Princess Pocahontas at Gravesend, understandably turning her back on the town

The author, walking near Shellhaven Creek

the mutt. Power-stations, airport schemes and even rubbish tips are all fine things in their way, but who wants to take a long walk through them?

There is, however, a second version of Thames Estuary that offers a very different prospect. This idealised and prettified version of the Thames Estuary is available to everybody, and it avoids all the flaws put in, whether deliberately or inadvertently, by the Almighty, when He laid out the original. Above all, it is only three quarters of a mile long.

Thames Estuary II is a series of landscaped canals, lakes and ponds, wrapped around the Bluewater shopping mall, one mile inland from the river. On 10 March 1999, the day that the Bluewater officially opened, I attended a press conference. "Why the name Bluewater?" someone had asked. "It evokes the majesty and flow of the River Thames, which the architect also reflects in the overall design of the centre," said the spokesman, in a line he obviously had off pat.

The press corps surged out to see the department stores, but hunt as I might, I couldn't find any scumbag raincoats. I soon tired of shopping, and went off to explore the walking instead.

Leaving the grand mall at the sector called Water Circus, I picked up the Bluewater canal where it winds beneath high chalk cliffs. These cliffs are more spectacular and precipitous by far than anything on the real-life Estuary (Bluewater is built in a worked-out chalk quarry). Just a few yards away from the giant shopping-mall, all was peaceful. Inside the futuristic structure, thousands of voices babbled away, and the tills shunted to and fro. On the canalside path, though, the only sounds were natural ones. A breeze wandered through the hundreds of pine trees that had been planted along the banks, causing the occasional stir. Immaculately groomed coots scuttled in and out of designer reed-beds. The clean, clear water looked as if it had been through my mum's washing-machine.

A red tarmac path crossed and re-crossed the water, constantly forming new vistas. After a while, the canal opened up into a sequence of lakes. Fountains bubbled at the side, cascades of rose-bushes were reflected in the waters, a waterfall trilled gently down depositing itself with a genteel splash into the lake. Lush green lawns, picked out with topiary hedges rolled down to the water's edge. So the paradisiacal mini-Estuary wends it way, until at last it plants you at one of the main entrances to the mall, all ready for some serious shopping. Etched into the entrance way are lines from Kipling: "As new flowers put forth to glad new men/ Out of the spent and unconsidered earth, the cities rise again." This, then, was the Estuary as art, an idealised vision crafted by a landscape architect who, no doubt very wisely, hadn't spent too much time staring at the real thing that lay just over the hill.

Yet, idyllic as it all was, the real, rough, crude Estuary still managed to make its presence felt. In unintended ways, the Bluewater waters had already started to reshape themselves in the style of the original model. For a start, just as with the real Estuary, the Bluewater path is a lonely place. I met just one other set of walkers, an elderly mid-European gentleman and his wife. "I see you like to walk too," he announced, even before I could accost him. "We are a privileged aristocracy, we walkers, we have all this to ourselves, yes, no," he said.

Then, right at the end of the River Bluewater, we made a discovery. Most of the waterway lives up to its name. Its base is that gleaming azure lining material, familiar from swimming pools and known amongst the disrespectful as "Hollywood flat bottom." With this blue binding to keep the water in, the Bluewater version of the Thames Estuary flowed clean and clear, if rather sterile. Yet, at the end, Nature had started to reassert herself. She did so in the way she knew best when it comes to canals, with mud. The silt had started to creep out into the waterway at a spot just beside the Pizza Express, hiding the dazzling blue bottom and choking the flow of the water. It was just a tiny aberration in an otherwise flawless landscape. Yet this mud-patch was still an assertion. Even in this place of

sophistication, artifice and big bucks, the spent and unconsidered earth could make a comeback if it chose. Or was this
touch of mud a deliberate landscape feature, a small tribute to
the true facts of the blue Estuary yonder?

Certainly the waters of Bluewater were an indication as to
what might also be done with the real Estuary one day, given a
bit of planting, a spot of land sculpting, and an influx of walkers and cyclists. First, though, people had to start to turn their
faces to it, and the key here was the path. "The path is what's
going to do it," the members of the Tilbury Action Group had
told me, in a place that now seemed to be a thousand miles
back. Well, the path was already there for the most part. It
could use a nice red tarmac top-dressing, like the path in
Bluewater. But at least it existed for the most part. It was an
unknown, unrecognised thread, but an Estuary passage for all
that. Secure in this knowledge, we set off on the last stage of
the walk.

On this final day, I inevitably cast my mind to that wedding
day, years before, when the Estuary had turned blue and sung:
"I am calling you-hoo-hoo-hoo." I had felt sure that it had some
message to offer, some great secret to disclose. Yet nothing had
materialised on this walk so far, other than a heightened aware-
ness of this neglected place's existence, and a magnificent natural history lesson that gave me an insight into the teeming life
of the mud. Not that this absence of revelation worried me.
The walk itself, with its constant surprises, had been justifica-
tion enough. What was more, in just three miles I would have
fulfilled a lifetime's ambition, and created my very own trail.
Still, another sign would be nice.

I had no sooner thought this, than my wish was granted,
although in a way that could only rebound embarrassingly.
What happened was that a crab waved at me. I recognised
immediately just how ridiculous I would look if I set this fact
down on record. Nobody would ever believe me. But there
could be no doubt as to the occurrence. Essex Dog had discov-

ered the crustacean, and was barking and whining at it. The crab, unperturbed, ignored the dog and looked straight at me. And waved. It wasn't a friendly sort of wave, more a traffic cop's gesture: "Come along now, get a move on there, stop gawping at me, you get on with your business and I'll get on with mine," it seemed to say. But I didn't move on. I stared at it in amazement, but all ready to make a scientific observation. I even thought that I recognised the type of crab. It was *Pagurus Bernhardus*. Laurence Watts and John Skinner had done their work well.

Alas, that one wave was all the sign that the Estuary or its wildlife was prepared to make. The rest was silence. Eventually, while I held Essex Dog's collar, the phlegmatic crab wandered off, in a perfectly ordinary manner, without calling further on its remarkable powers of communication. Then the Dog and I also wandered off, in the direction demanded by the crab. If I had realised that this sea creature was trying to kill me, I might have acted rather differently.

For the first mile out of Sheerness, the path marched on toward Estuary's end on a sturdy, concrete base. Just past the village of Minster, the bungalows drew back from the water's edge. Now there were just the Estuary, the dog and me, alone with one another. At this point, the sturdy concrete path ended. So did the map in my little "Local Red" book of street maps. We were entering uncharted territory. This did not worry me. I was sure that I would recognise Warden Point when I saw it. I had been contemplating its otter's head shape for enough years. So we strode unconcernedly along the bare foreshore. It was here, at the end of civilisation, that the cliffs and the troubles commenced.

I was aware within seconds that this stretch of shore was different from anything I had ever tried to walk before. This was a terrain where human beings had just given up trying. Within the first few yards I was sinking up to my calves in mud. This mud was quite unlike the normal, beloved Estuary stuff in which the little sea creatures romped and rogered. This was a sinister, glutinous ooze. Belonging neither to the land nor the water, it seemed to be more powerful than either. The slime was made up of the putrefying remnants of what had been, not so long ago, cliffs – the very sea-cliffs that had mesmerised me down the years as I looked across from the other side of the Estuary. On top of this morass, the carcases of maimed trees and shredded bushes rotted into the mud. Glutinous, clayey puddles, parodies of normal rock-pools, filled out the odd pouch in the mud. The whole Passchendaele-like scene was overlaid by the stink of dead and dying land. And scattered here and there were the saddest remnants of all – chunks of concrete, the size of small cars, that had once been part of a scenic concrete walkway. The mudquake seemed to have reserved its greatest frenzy for this presumptuous path.

I had done quite a few stories about coastal erosion, and I knew about the theory of limited surrender to the sea. In some places it was simply deemed too expensive to build sea defences. In any case, better to let the sea have its way. What it stole in one place, it deposited somewhere else. People whose land and homes were actually being nicked by the oceans, tend to disagree, and wail in protest. But the prevailing ethos remains. Let the land go, let the sea have its will, especially in sparsely populated places like north-east Sheppey. All of this appears politic enough, if rather sad, when talked about in theory. Coastal erosion was something I had always talked about over a telephone or round a desk, a few miles safely inland. None of this had quite prepared me for the horrific reality of this hideous, shattered landscape.

At least I should have known better than to try to walk through it. The alternative route, was along the cliff-top, out of sight but just sixty feet above my head. This, though, was even less promising. It consisted of endless caravan-parks, serviced by a single, narrow lane. This was no way to end the Estuary trail, pressed into the side of a hedge, watching as a speeding

camper-van pancaked Essex Dog. I had got this far, and I was-
n't going to become part of the surrender to coastal erosion, not
with just two miles to go. In any case, if the mud was that dangerous, there would have been warning signs. In retrospect,
there almost certainly were – perhaps many. But these signposts
must simply have been smashed and slubbed away along with
anything else that stood in the way of the shifting mud.

And so we set out along the pulp that passed for a foreshore.
Essex Dog had recently been placed on an enforced diet, and
she skipped nimbly enough across the mud. She even managed
to set off a couple of small landslides. But for me, every step was
a heave. There were constant detours round giant potholes and
gashes, numerous retreats from what looked like safe ground,
but turned out to be treacherous black glue. I had travelled no
more than a few hundred yards through this slough, when I
knew that I was beaten. The choice lay between turning back
or climbing the cliff. I knew what lay in store just from the simple act of retracing my footsteps, and the prospect almost made
me sick. So I decided on the second choice, and started to
climb the cliff. The ascent looked easy enough. It was the sight
of a recent landslide, a six-foot wide river of mud, fresh enough
not to have been colonised by algae. In theory, I could just follow this gravy stain to the top of the cliff, and blessedly firm
ground. All prejudice gone, I vowed to kiss the first caravan
that I met, however much indignation it caused the owner. So
I began to climb, and after just a few feet I became well and
truly stuck.

I subsided in slow motion. My boot sank, my trouser-calf
sank, and still the sinking continued, with me on top vaguely
wondering when it was all going to stop. I eventually ceased
this downward motion at knee level, well and truly bedded into
that decaying cliff face. To make matters worse, Essex Dog con-
cluded that all this was some bright new game, devised for her
benefit. She began to prance round me, barking and snapping
at where my ankles would normally have been, represented in

their absence by my hips and bottom. I could only envy her the freedom of movement.

I made a supreme effort to haul my leg out of the mire, but I was already exhausted, and this effort just left me panting. "Don't panic," I told myself. I wasn't panicking, but I was worn down in body and spirit, flummoxed – and still stuck.

I was buoyed up by one thought. Whatever sort of quandary I was in, this figured as the ultimate, all-time Frustration Walk. Once again, Kent had beaten Essex. Nothing on the north side of the Estuary could match the perfection with which this liquid Kentish clay stymied any passage of any sort. There and then I awarded this so-called trail a record 1,000 frustration points. Only a path that actually killed was likely to gain more.

For a few minutes, Essex Dog and I basked in the sunshine on the edge of the cliff, enjoying the novel tanning position. But something had to be done to release me from the cliff's grip. Then came the motivation.

It took the form of a tree, a hawthorn that, like me, was embedded in the landslide. It was still upright, and unlike the shattered trees at the foot of the cliffs, still very much alive and in full green leaf. It was also moving. The movement was definite, if glacier-paced. There was no doubt that this tree was sliding downhill even if it took twelve months or more to arrive at the beach. And it was aiming straight at me. It was moving and I was not, so sooner or later, if I remained here, that hawthorn was going to have me.

The thought of being mugged by a tree gave me the surge of muscle power that I needed. With one slurp I was free. I began to descend again. A second later I was stuck once more. It took another massive wrench to get free again. By any standards, this was a slow-motion descent. At this rate, the tree was almost certainly moving faster than I was.

I could feel the hot breath of the hawthorn on my neck by the time I reached the bottom. Now I was well and truly marooned. Ascent was impossible, and I lacked the energy to crawl back the way I had come. There and then, I decided that I had had enough. I was going to call for help. I would ring my wife, and, as usual, pass the buck to her. While she called out the emergency services, and the Sheppey abseilers prepared for action, I was going to have a sleep.

I rummaged into the rucksack for the mobile phone. But where was it? I found my lunchbox, my maps, Essex Dog's supplies, and half of an old plate, decorated with mermaids, that I had found on the beach. But no Nokia. Either it had dropped into the mud, perhaps to be picked up by some other beach-comber fifty years from now. Or, more likely, one of the kids had filched it. Whatever the reason, I was truly in a plight.

Can there be anything more naked and exposed than modern man without his mobile? Just a few hours ago, I had been a cocky and swaggering creature of the telecommunications age, sneering my way through Sheerness. No matter what stupid things I did, a quick word into Mr Nokia's chip-carton would sort out any problems. Now I was primitive man, cowering in this savage, shattered world of shifting clay and empty horizons. I was Swanscombe Man (male version), I was a Neanderthal oyster-gatherer. No, I was worse than that. In the absence of a Swiss Army penknife, I wouldn't know how to open and eat a bloody oyster if one jumped in my hand.

The world had been reduced to mud, sea and a hazy view of Southend, which now looked more beautiful and alluring across the Estuary than Sheppey had ever done. Not only was there no sign of humanity, there was never going to be any sign of humanity, not for years. I had called the marshes wilderness, but they were Piccadilly compared to this mud-beach. Nobody was ever going to visit this foul, broken place.

There remained the ships, entering and leaving the Thames at its juncture with the wide world. They were three miles out, as remote and inaccessible as distant planets. They plied their business, as detached and aloof from the Estuary on which they rode as everybody else.

Even so, I waved wildly at them, in a desperate bid to attract some sort of human attention. What, though, would ships' passengers and crew make of this mud-smeared barbarian, prancing and gesturing at them. "The English population really is going to the dogs," they would think.

Was this the mystery that the Estuary had promised to unlock? Had I been staring across the Estuary, all those years, at a vision of my own demise? The affection for this place that had built up over 83 miles began to change to hatred. "You tricked me, you bastard," I thought to the Estuary. "No wonder people despise you."

Yet perhaps I only had myself to blame. I had tried to beat a path round the Estuary, to trap it, to make it fit for mild ramblers like myself and Essex Dog. Was it any wonder that the Estuary had bitten back? The Estuary wasn't going to be tamed by any circular path. It was on the move, hungry to forge more sea. An estuary is a balance between land and water. If you spend your life on solid ground, you fondly imagine that it is the land that is boss. Crouching where I crouched, looking at the smashed walkway and the convulsed, tortured cliffs, there could be no such delusion. The sea had tired of harmonious co-existence and was on the march, pulping the land into this terrible mud, more inhospitable as a human environment than ice, more vengeful than lava. This was the shape of the end of the world, and it already existed, here at the end of the Thames and the world. At last I had got the message. Only now it looked as if it was too late to pass it on.

It was then, as I crouched, bewildered and beaten in the mud, that the Estuary made the last of all its gestures to me. It could have struck me down. Instead, it drew its sting. What happened was quite unexpected and unlooked for, but it saved the day.

As I looked despairingly across the Estuary, and even, madly, began to wonder whether it wouldn't be best to swim for it, the tide began to go out. I hadn't even thought of consulting any tide-tables before I set out that morning. On this occasion, though, the Estuary had timed itself to be onside.

The waning of the tide exposed a stretch of relatively clear mud, scoured flat by the sea, glistening, and clean. Carefully, I stepped out on it. The mud-way was clear of obstacles, and, while still soft, a good deal more walkable than the beach. It seemed to offer a clear, if slow, path to safety.

The prudent course of action would have been to head back to Sheerness as fast as possible. I wasn't going to do that, however. The Estuary had presented me with this last stretch of makeshift trail, and boy, was I going to make use of it. So, with infinite care, I inched my way toward Warden Point.

In the end, we almost tiptoed straight past it. Warden Point, which appears so distinctive, dark and mysterious from a distance, is none of these things when you stand on or beneath it. Nor, for a Point, is it very pointed. How typical of the Estuary that its Kentish tip should be so easily missed.

The dog and I barely gave Warden Point a second glance. It was only the appearance of some other humans on the cliff-top that stopped us in our tracks. I was mighty pleased to see some fellow creatures. At this point, the cliff had turned into a slope. I found that it was possible to scramble upward without too much difficulty. Waving and yelling at the human beings, I made my way up toward them as fast as possible.

The little group looked understandably apprehensive at the appearance of this muddy apparition, rising up from the no man's land of the beach. They turned out to be a party of active pensioners from a retirement home in Margate. Whatever their circumstances, I noticed that they possessed something that I did not – a proper Ordnance Survey map.

"Do you know if this is Warden Point?" I asked.

"That's right," said the man with the map. "Beginning and end of the world they call it."

"Load of old ****, I call it," said another pensioner. He seemed a disagreeable fellow, but he had a point. Warden Point consisted of some abandoned cottages, a dead tree, a pot-holed lane and a pair of concrete bollards. It wasn't really the stuff of which Meccas are made.

"We've been making day trips along the coast," said map-man. "Got to prove there's life in the old dog yet, not let them tie you down drinking tea with the ladies all day, haven't you."

"Quite right," I said. "Are you going any further?"

"We thought we'd try to walk our way along the Estuary. But it's a bit difficult. There aren't really any guides available to it."

"Tell me about it," I said.

The pensioners headed back for their car. I stopped for a last commune with the Estuary. There was going to be no more shore walking today. I was going to take the country lane to the nearest telephone box, and call a taxi.

First, however, we stood to savour our achievement. Or, at least, I did. Essex Dog simply curled up and went to sleep.

The Estuary was looking its most benign. While nowhere approaching the rich blue that I had seen from the terrace of the yacht club, it was at least a welcoming shade of grey. "Me? I wouldn't hurt a fly," it seemed to say.

Yet this is the Estuary that sooner or later will wash us all away. This realisation was the highlight of my career. I had scooped the ultimate end of the world story. But all that was to be written about and worried about some other day. Meanwhile, I realised that the Estuary had taught me another, and very sim-ple, truth (apart from: Don't forget your mobile phone). It went like this:

There is more fun to be had alongside the Thames Estuary than you might think.

At least we appreciated this now. But had I missed anything else? I prodded Essex Dog awake. There were more stories and endless revelations, as well as obvious truths, to be had out there on unfashionable Thameside. We turned round, and began to walk back along the Estuary in reverse, just one more time.